W9-CLC-630

Praise for *All Students Must Thrive*

"*All Students Must Thrive* is the book we need right now. There is growing awareness that by focusing narrowly on student achievement we have ignored the social and emotional needs of too many children. As a result, the children with the greatest needs are usually the ones who do least well in school. This book provides practical insights on how to reverse that tendency by incorporating a focus on the social and emotional needs of children into our classrooms and school so that all children can indeed thrive."—Pedro A. Noguera, PhD, Distinguished Professor of Education, faculty director, Center for the Transformation of Schools

"*All Students Must Thrive: Transforming Schools to Combat Toxic Stressors and Cultivate Critical Wellness* is a brilliantly constructed manual for deliberately combatting the pervasive layers of oppression that permeate school practices, structures, and systems—and ourselves—and that harm our young people. It makes clear that caring for youth requires centering relationships and an intentional focus on critical wellness. The impressive team of authors brings a wealth of experience and expertise to the project of transformation that must begin with each of us and that must also be collective and systemic work. Each writer argues convincingly for a key element of the kaleidoscope of action necessary to adopt a critical wellness framework rooted in the tenets of critical pedagogy and critical race theory. The book offers thoughtful support for action to disrupt patterns of racism and oppression without detaching the practical from the theoretical. The authors deftly interweave theory, history, and critical analysis with practice and the result is a book rich in resources that meets each reader where they are. They provide language to use, scenarios to consider, questions for the field to take up, beginning steps on how to do this challenging work, and support for learning and action. This is a seminal text that every educator must study and use to develop themselves and their practice, as individuals and as members of communities."—Deborah Loewenberg Ball, William H. Payne Collegiate Professor in Education and Arthur F. Thurnau Professor; director, TeachingWorks; research professor, Institute for Social Research

"Tyrone Howard and his author team have helped many of our nation's educators grow their skills and understanding, so that schools are equitable places. *All Students Must Thrive* provides straightforward structures and strategies for identifying both intentional and unintentional ideologies, theories, practices, and policies that contribute to inequities. The authors also share insights on how to best combat these inequities. A must-read for those committed to assisting *all* children to become *all* they are capable of being."—Bill Daggett, founder and chairman, International Center for Leadership in Education

"Over the last several years, massive breakthroughs have been happening across fields like neuroscience, physiology, and social epidemiology that have exploded our thinking about how radicalized inequality and toxic stress affect the well-being of our young people. These findings often echo the best teachings of our ancestors, which have been largely ignored, and have led to important shifts in the conversation about meeting the needs of vulnerable and wounded students. Tyrone Howard and his coauthors have been on the leading edge of those conversations because they are on the ground, doing the work directly with the students and teachers that are most urgently in need of our support. For that reason, *All Students Must Thrive* is an essential volume for all those that call themselves concerned with the youth and families that our school systems have continuously failed to serve."—Jeff Duncan-Andrade, PhD, associate professor, Raza Studies & Education, San Francisco State University

"In *All Students Must Thrive*, Dr. Howard and his coauthors affirm, with grace and clarity, what educators, activists, and Black and Brown communities have long felt in their bones: that to educate a student is to acknowledge, celebrate, and uplift their complex racial and cultural identities. The strategies and insights offered in this volume to advance that understanding by elevating the field's cultural awareness are elegant and informed by the team's unparalleled expertise and collective decades of education practitioner experience. Our work in New Jersey is focusing on transformation, including forging a culture of high expectations and diversifying our teaching force. These initiatives, in tandem with our embrace of a whole-child approach to education through enhancing social and emotional learning, help ensure that all students succeed in school and in life. In this book, Dr. Howard and his team offer insights and recommendations to support this most fundamental need. I am hopeful that all other educators concerned with democratizing access to high-quality education for students of all races, cultures, and lived experiences will do well to consider the practices and understandings shared in this work."—Commissioner Lamont O. Repollet, EdD, New Jersey Department of Education

All Students Must Thrive

Transforming Schools to Combat Toxic Stressors and Cultivate Critical Wellness

Tyrone C. Howard

Patrick Camangian, Earl J. Edwards, Maisah Howard, Andréa C. Minkoff, Tonikiaa Orange, Jonli D. Tunstall, Kenjus T. Watson

FOREWORD BY H. RICHARD MILNER IV

International Center for
Leadership in Education.

From Houghton Mifflin Harcourt.

International Center for Leadership in Education, Inc.
1587 Route 146
Rexford, New York 12148
www.LeaderEd.com
info@LeaderEd.com

Copyright © 2019 by International Center for Leadership in Education, a division of
Houghton Mifflin Harcourt Publishing Company.

All rights reserved.

No part of this publication may be reproduced in whole or in part, or stored in a
retrieval system, or transmitted in any form or by any means, electronic, mechanical,
photocopying, recording, or otherwise, without written permission of the publisher.
Requests for permission to make copies of any part of the work should be addressed
to Houghton Mifflin Harcourt Publishing Company, Attn: Contracts, Copyrights, and
Licensing, 9400 South Park Center Loop, Orlando, Florida 32819

ISBN: 978-1-328-02704-7

International Center For Leadership In Education
is a division of Houghton Mifflin Harcourt.

INTERNATIONAL CENTER FOR LEADERSHIP IN EDUCATION® and associated
logos are trademarks or registered trademarks of Houghton Mifflin Harcourt Publishing
Company. Other company names, brand names, and product names are the property and/
or trademarks of their respective owners.

Figure 2.1. Copyright © 2019 by Maisah Howard.
Figure 2.2. Copyright © ericsphotography/Getty Images—
Portrait of local girl in red and white tank top.

Printed in the United States of America.

3 4 5 6 7 8 9 10 0304 28 27 26 25 24 23 22 21 20

4510006938 ABCD

Contents

Acknowledgments

A project such as this does not come to fruition without numerous tireless advocates and supporters. The contributors to this book are indebted to countless individuals who support us in our efforts to do the work of equity, healing, and transforming schools and communities. The work of wellness can at times be physically, mentally, and emotionally challenging. We are fortunate to have people who have held us up when the burdens of this work often feel the heaviest. First and foremost, we thank our respective families. The unwavering love, support, queries, conversations, and encouragement of our families in this work are highly valued and deeply appreciated. Whether it was our children, spouses, parents, grandparents, siblings, nieces, nephews, cousins, in-laws, or close friends, each of our respective villages are our foundation. We thank all of you for understanding our relentless pursuit of justice, recognizing our crazy schedules, but always believing in our ability to make a difference in our world.

Second, we have all had the good fortune of working with numerous friends, current and former students, coworkers, colleagues, as well as writing and thought partners who help us in this work every day. Having a community to help you do this work is important, necessary, and fortifying. We appreciate those individuals who are our critical friends.

Finally, we express our deepest gratitude to the districts, schools, administrators, teachers, counselors, staff, and students who allow us to come into their arena to do this work. We learn through every exchange, each idea, occasional disagreements, and ongoing discussions that you have shared with us. We are appreciative of those schools trusting each of us to impart wisdom, share experiences and practices, offer insights, challenge thinking, and provide knowledge strategies and suggestions to make our schools and communities better. Our goal is to create healing spaces in all schools, which will expand to permeate families, communities, our nation, and ultimately our global village. Not only do we have a professional obligation to make schools better places, but we see this as our personal imperative and hold the deep-seated, unwavering conviction that all children must receive nothing less than loving, affirming, intellectually stimulating, and welcoming schools.

About the Authors

Patrick Camangian, PhD, is an associate professor in the Department of Teacher Education and coordinator of the Urban Education and Social Justice Credential and Master's program at the University of San Francisco School of Education. His scholarship examines critical pedagogy and transformative teaching in urban schools, action research, critical literacy, culturally empowering education, and urban teacher development. Currently, he is turning to both critical theory and research in the health sciences to inform his research findings on complex traumas and urban education. Camangian has been an English teacher since 1999, continuing in the tradition of teacher research, applying critical pedagogies in urban schools.

Earl J. Edwards is a doctoral student in the Graduate School of Education & Information Studies at UCLA. Earl is a former homeless youth and currently researches how teachers and administrators identify, support, and educate students dealing with social emotional trauma. Prior to attending UCLA, Earl was a high school special education teacher and received his master's degree from Teachers College, Columbia University in Public School Administration.

Maisah Howard, MEd, MSW, is a former children's social worker with the Los Angeles County Department of Children and Family Services. She has worked in child welfare for over twenty-three years, working with children and families to keep children safe, engage extended family to secure lifelong connections for youth, coordinate necessary resources, and help to remediate the need for child welfare interventions. Maisah is also a former elementary school classroom teacher who taught in the Compton Unified School District. Maisah has provided professional development for teachers, staffs, and administrators nationally, focusing on ways to support the needs of children and families dealing with social emotional trauma.

Tyrone C. Howard, PhD, is a professor in the Graduate School of Education & Information Studies at UCLA. Howard is also the inaugural director of the new UCLA Pritzker Center for Strengthening Children and Families, a campus-wide consortium examining academic, mental health, and social emotional experiences and challenges for California's most vulnerable youth populations. He is also the former associate dean for equity, diversity, and inclusion. Howard's research examines culture, race, teaching, and learning. He has published over seventy-five peer-reviewed journal articles, book chapters, and technical reports. He has published several best-selling books, among them *Why Race and Culture Matter in Schools* and *Black Male(d): Peril and Promise in the Education of African American Males.* His most recent book, *Expanding College Access for Urban Youth* (Teachers College Press, 2016), documents ways that schools and colleges can create higher education opportunities for youth of color. Howard is also the director and founder of the Black Male Institute at UCLA, an interdisciplinary cadre of scholars, practitioners, community members, and policymakers dedicated to examining the nexus of race, class, and gender in relation to school-age youth. A native and former classroom teacher in Compton, California, Howard was named the recipient of the 2015 UCLA Distinguished Teaching Award, which is the university's highest honor for teaching excellence. In 2016, Howard was listed by *Education Week* as one of the fifty most influential scholars in the nation informing educational policy, practice, and reform.

Andréa C. Minkoff, PhD, is an alumna of the Graduate School of Education & Information Studies at UCLA, having earned her PhD in education with an emphasis in urban schooling. Prior to that, she earned her preliminary multiple-subject credential, MAT, and BA from Occidental College. Her research interests include teachers' work and lives, children's understandings of race and gender, children's language ideologies, literacy as a social process, and intergroup relations and identity development in the context of school. She has taught undergraduate and master's students at both Occidental College and Chapman University.

Tonikiaa Orange, PhD, is a former classroom teacher and principal. She has taught in the Graduate School of Education & Information Studies at UCLA for the past ten years, where she teaches preservice teachers and principals in training. Her work has paid particular attention to the role of culture and cognition. Her work also addresses the alignment of curricular goals and objectives with cultural content and knowledge. She has been a professional development provider focusing on culturally and linguistically responsive pedagogy for the Los Angeles Unified School District; Minneapolis Public Schools; Normandy School District in Ferguson, Missouri; and multiple school districts in northern California, such as Castro Valley, San Ramon, and Hayward.

Jonli D. Tunstall, PhD, has, over the course of her fourteen-year tenure at UCLA, served in a number of formal and informal positions that have contributed to the acceptance and graduation of underrepresented students across the country. In her current role as a member of the senior leadership team in the UCLA Academic Advancement Program (AAP), Jonli oversees several programs and initiatives that work with first-generation, low-income, underrepresented students. Currently she directs two programs as part of the AAP team: VIP Scholars, a social justice college access program, and the freshman and transfer summer program. She also teaches courses in the African American Studies, Education, and Ethnomusicology Departments, and is the cofounder of the Sister-to-Sister Institute, which addresses the specific needs related to the retention and socialization of African American women at historically White institutions. Her extensive background in higher education, college access, and retention has enabled her to serve on a number of university and community-based committees working to impact the K–16 education system and diversify institutions of higher education.

Kenjus T. Watson, PhD, teaches courses on educational inequality, urban education, critical race theory, and social identity and group behavior in the Education Department at Occidental College. Prior to joining the faculty in the Education Department, Kenjus served as the assistant director of the Intergroup Dialogue Program and a faculty member in the Psychology Department at Occidental, where he has worked for the past five years. Kenjus has been involved with intergroup dialogue and other forms of social justice education in higher and secondary education for over a decade and has established dialogue programs at several universities across the country.

Kenjus's scholarship investigates issues of race, racism, and other aspects of oppression found throughout the educational pipeline. His current research interests focus on the biopsychosocial impact of racial microaggressions in higher education, the history of racial microaggressions research, critical race theory, Black collegiate identities, and the potential of critical pedagogy to inspire action, hope, and healing among marginalized communities. Kenjus has collaborated with over thirty institutions and organizations within K–12 and higher education settings in implementing assessments and developing capacity to work mindfully on issues of social justice.

About the International Center for Leadership in Education

The International Center for Leadership in Education (ICLE), a division of Houghton Mifflin Harcourt, challenges, inspires, and equips leaders and teachers to prepare their students for lifelong success. At the heart of all we do is the proven philosophy that the entire system must be aligned around instructional excellence—rooted in rigor, relevance, and relationships—to ensure that every student is prepared for a successful future.

Founded in 1991 by Dr. Bill Daggett, ICLE, through its team of thought leaders and consultants, helps schools and districts bring innovative practices to scale through professional learning opportunities and coaching partnerships guided by the cornerstones of our work: the Daggett System for Effective Instruction® and the Rigor/Relevance Framework®. In addition, ICLE shares successful practices that have a positive impact on student learning, through keynote presentations; the Model Schools Conference, Leadership Academy, and other events; and a rich collection of publications. Learn more at LeaderEd.com.

Foreword

D rawing from extensive, varied and relevant experiences, these authors show us the possibilities of educational equity and justice when educators decide to notice instead of judging, care rather than criticizing, and pursue wellness over pathologizing. *All Students Must Thrive* is an extremely important and excellent book that focuses on structural, institutional, systemic, and individual challenges we face in education in our quest to teach and support the whole child. The authors place, front and center, the critical need for those in education to understand and respond to students and educators' psychological, social, and emotional wellness and humanity. A fine balance of insights and recommendations for student and adult development, we read in this book how living and learning in racist, sexist, homophobic, xenophobic and otherwise discriminatory contexts, inside and outside of school, can result in various forms of toxicity, which have been shown to result in increased stress, anxiety, depression, and trauma writ large.

This book demonstrates that it is difficult to teach subject matter to any group of students in any school context without deeply interrogating and building tools to teach to and through the psychological, social, and emotional health of students. Readers are introduced to elements of what the authors conceptualize as *critical wellness*. Critical wellness is advanced as a necessity for educators and others who work in educational contexts with students whose social, emotional, and political landscapes have worked against them, their families, and their communities. Indeed, as the authors have conceptualized it, anyone working with young people from camp counselors to social workers to school educators should press toward critical wellness. When critical wellness becomes part of our educational ethos, students and educators alike benefit because they work concurrently toward healing and humanization. As a pedagogical stance and an outcome, the authors advance humanization as an essential tenet of critical wellness. In the authors' words: "Humanization as a critically relevant, and real, form of social and emotional health and well-being, must channel the hurt and desire of students to express the pathos of community suffering that too often goes unacknowledged."

Thus, drawing from research literature, the authors offer optimistic views, insights, and recommendations of what is possible in our quest to support and care for the humanity and the humanization of all students inside and outside of school. Indeed, the book advances an optimistic agenda of transformation, one that leaves readers with not only a call to do better but overt examples of what we can and should do to build knowledge and understanding of Black and Brown students, students whose first language is not English, students experiencing homelessness, and students who live below the poverty line. Cornel West wrote in the preface of the important book *Restoring Hope: Conversations on the Future of Black America*:

> Hope is not the same as optimism. Optimism adopts the role of the spectator who surveys the evidence in order to infer that things are going to get better . . . Hope enacts the stance of the participant who *actively struggles* [emphasis added] against the evidence in order to change the deadly tides of wealth inequality, group xenophobia, and personal despair. Only a new wave of vision, courage, and hope can keep us sane—and preserve the decency and dignity requisite to revitalize our organizational energy for the work to be done. To live is to wrestle with despair yet never to allow despair to have the last word. (p. xii)

What might happen when teachers and other educators are prepared and equipped with tools to support students whose psychological, social, and emotional needs are viewed as essential to their academic success? How can we support educators in building the knowledge, attitudes, and understandings necessary to identify and respond to students' traumatic, grieving, and psychologically strained situations? Moreover, what might happen if students who are placed on the margins of learning, those whom schools most often give up on, are understood as human beings—worthy and deserving of educational facilities, institutions, and educators of excellence? This book graces readers with eight chapters that draw from and on story, research, and promising practices that address these and so many other relevant and interrelated questions.

An invitation to push past the obvious and a call to learn with students about the intersections of mental health, trauma, and education, this book teaches as it heals and humanizes.

—H. Richard Milner IV, Cornelius Vanderbilt
Professor of Education,
Vanderbilt University

Reference

West, C. (1997). Preface. In K. S. Sealey (Ed.), *Restoring hope: Conversations on the future of Black America*. Boston: Beacon Press.

Introduction

For educators, one of the core challenges today is eradicating chronic disparities and accumulative disadvantages that often appear unrelenting, are historical in nature, and are major obstacles for teaching and learning. A number of topics have been discussed to ameliorate academic disparities for low-income and racially diverse students. Topics related to school choice, charter schools, teacher preparation, parent engagement, early childhood education, and curricular and instructional approaches have all been extensively dissected and debated as ways to improve school outcomes for students of color.

What has not been as prevalent in the school reform discussion is the persistent impact of various toxic stressors that influence students' opportunities to learn. Issues such as trauma, anxiety, abuse, neglect, discrimination, racism, and depression are typically not offered as explanations for why certain students do not thrive in school.

It's time to change this discourse.

All Students Must Thrive is intended to inform educators about social and economic issues—trauma, death, violence, displacement, abuse, and racism—that have a profound impact on students' social emotional well-being and their ability to learn in schools. *Critical wellness* in education is a concept that addresses the role of race, culture, trauma, mental health, social emotional* well-being, bias, identity, and adverse circumstances that inhibit students' ability to be whole in the pursuit of education. And it does so without placing these issues within a deficit-laden framework that blames children, families, and communities for their circumstances. This book argues that the concept of critical wellness is vital to correcting school inequity. It also provides strategies for implementing a critical wellness framework in a class, a classroom, a school, or throughout a school district.

*The terms *social and emotional* and *social emotional* will be used interchangeably.

A Critical Wellness Framework

There is a need to profoundly change how educators understand the historical, structural, and political factors that create and sustain deep-seated inequities in schools and society. These inequities have a devastating effect on children and their capacity to learn. The literature on wellness has centered on approaches to optimum levels of health, social and emotional functioning, and cognitive well-being that help individuals grow and thrive. At the center of much of the literature on wellness is the integration of the body, mind, and spirit as a means of achieving peak development, as well as the appreciation that everything one does, thinks, feels, and believes has an impact on the state of one's overall health.

These core aspects of wellness are vital to living and learning, but they fail to take into account students' identities and social and economic realities, which are equally vital to development. Frequently absent from the wellness literature is an acknowledgment that such issues as poverty, race, gender identity, and structural inequities act as impediments for many students in schools. To amend this shortfall, critical wellness in education brings together three theoretical frameworks that have relevance for equity in schools: *wellness, critical pedagogy*, and *critical race theory.*

The World Health Organization (WHO) describes wellness as "a state of complete physical, mental, and social well-being, and not merely the absence of disease or infirmity." Wellness is also tied to the concept of seeking optimal health in the connection between mind, body, and spirit. As the WHO definition explicitly states, wellness is not the mere absence of disease. It is a proactive, preventive, and radical approach designed to achieve high levels of health and social and emotional functioning, which in turn can improve learning outcomes for our most vulnerable student populations. In the context of education, wellness also encompasses whole-child education and is closely related to the theory of "overlapping spheres." The concept of whole-child education and the theory of overlapping spheres are heavily influential in the outcomes of all children, but have increased significance for youth who live in more challenging circumstances. Whole-child education works specifically to provide health, wellness, and academically and socially enriching resources and services to young people. *All Students Must Thrive* is concerned with this very issue: wellness for students to enable them to thrive socially, emotionally, culturally, and academically. But this wellness model has limitations—it fails to address issues with access, equity, and oppression.

Critical pedagogy operates from a tradition that has sought to raise important questions about access, equity, and the humanization process for marginalized populations. Critical pedagogy seeks to humanize through a critical examination of structural inequities that have plagued low-income communities of color for centuries. The authors of *All Students Must Thrive* seek to radically imagine schools in a way that offers a critique of social, political, and economic structures that influence students' lives in harmful ways. Thus an understanding of the effects of poverty and trauma is vital to improving educational outcomes because they explain much of what is witnessed in schools today.

Coupled with wellness and critical pedagogy, race is also important in understanding inequities in schools and classrooms. Within the field of education, critical race theory has become an evolving methodological, conceptual, and theoretical construct that seeks to disrupt race and racism in educational theory and practice. It enables scholars to ask, in unique ways, the important question of what racism has to do with inequities in education. Critical race theory also calls for an analysis of racism and its intersection with other forms of oppression, such as sexism, classism, homophobia, and nativism.

Together, these three theoretical models—wellness, critical pedagogy, and critical race theory—create the underpinnings of critical wellness. *All Students Must Thrive* was written from a standpoint that until educators develop knowledge, sensibilities, and strategies that are steeped in understanding students' realities, school transformation will remain elusive. Moreover, the chapters in this book are intentional in that they don't subscribe to simplistic understandings of real challenges students encounter daily in schools and society. Instead, we, the authors, highlight theoretical and practical considerations that should be contemplated in today's educational context for racially, linguistically, and culturally diverse students.

Knowledge and Strategies for All Educators

Although *All Students Must Thrive* has a strong theoretical grounding, the target audience is all K–12 educators whose work is directly concerned with marginalized populations, including teachers, teacher leaders, administrators, instructional coaches, and professional developers. Even though each classroom and school is unique, the presented strategies are useful in all educational environments and situations. And because the book is solution oriented in its approach and focus, it will also appeal to professional learning practitioners and professional learning communities. In addition, professors and students at schools of education will find many of the real-world scenarios useful in developing a deeper understanding of the complex and enduring issues that influence the ability to effectively teach today's student population.

Straightforward Structure, Practical Features

All Students Must Thrive consists of eight chapters written by experts in various areas of education. Each chapter offers a particular focus on ideology, theory, practice, or policy as a way to better support students of color, particularly in low-income schools. To start, chapter 1 sheds light on the importance of race and culture and how it influences teaching and learning. More pointedly, this chapter discusses why educators at all levels must develop racial awareness and cultural competence to understand the needs of today's learners.

Chapter 2 examines trauma, how it affects students in schools, and how it has a direct influence on wellness. A growing body of research has identified complex trauma to be a major impediment to wellness for students. One of the goals of this chapter is to familiarize readers with the terminology and work related to adverse childhood experiences (ACEs).

Chapter 3 introduces readers to the theoretical and pedagogical underpinnings of implicit bias and racial microaggressions in the classroom. This chapter outlines the current sociopolitical context of racial disparities in schools and offers a compelling rationale for engaging these precarious realities honestly and courageously.

In chapter 4, readers will learn how educators understand and implement culturally and linguistically responsive pedagogy (CLR) in the classroom. CLR brings to light the importance of delivering culturally authentic learning opportunities for diverse students and focuses on how altering a deficit mindset is needed in order to eliminate barriers to success for culturally and linguistically diverse students. In this chapter, readers will learn how teachers interpret, analyze, and resolve tensions in practice by being able to identify and remedy oppressive and culturally biased instruction and policies.

Chapter 5 contributes to the broader discussion of critical wellness in education by examining the role of student identity in shaping classroom culture and experiences in the primary grades. Early childhood educators are often the first adults in institutional settings to influence young children. Although research has shown both short- and long-term benefits to be associated with high-quality early childhood education, less is known about preparing effective early childhood educators, especially in the areas of diversity and identity.

Chapter 6 provides an overview of the challenges in creating college-going cultures. In so doing, it discusses ways to implement college and career readiness school-wide. This chapter lays out the sociocultural supports that impact academic success, as well as the role of care, high expectations, and culturally responsive pedagogy in preparing students for college and for a career.

In chapter 7, the focus is on how self-awareness, self-management, social awareness, relationship building, responsible decision-making, and self-efficacy relate to both the social alienation and social transformation of historically marginalized communities. In essence, this chapter examines the ways that social and emotional learning can challenge social alienation by teaching students about self, solidarity, and self-determination.

Finally, chapter 8 raises awareness of the growing number of students experiencing homelessness. This chapter seeks to equip readers with the knowledge and strategies necessary to ensure that all students—stably housed or not—have access to a high-quality learning experience.

To help practitioners render theory and research applicable in their classrooms or other educational settings, every chapter includes the following practical features:

- "Key Takeaways" to help the reader review and reference critical chapter points
- "Questions from the Field" to address the most common issues and queries from real-world educators
- "Recommended Resources" to help guide deeper study of chapter topics

- Real-world examples and vignettes that illustrate specific theories or strategies

In collaborating on this book, all of the authors worked from a simple supposition: educators will not maximize school outcomes for their most marginalized populations until they begin to better understand how the social emotional well-being of students profoundly influences learning. Collectively, we argue that responsively transforming schools requires an empathetic approach to teaching and learning that explicitly puts a focus on race, racism, trauma, mental health, and poverty. Moreover, this approach places a particular focus on how students of color are affected by these factors in their pursuit of education.

The needs of today's student population are diverse and complex. When situating opportunities to learn at the nexus of race and socioeconomic status, schools play a pivotal role in either deepening these challenges or alleviating them. Although the focus on testing and accountability has eased up somewhat in the last several years, pressure to improve student outcomes remains. Along with this emphasis on accountability, however, has been an unprecedented increase in racial and ethnic diversity in the nation's schools. In short, race still matters when discussing educational equity. Examining the intersection of race, trauma, poverty, and social emotional well-being is key to enhancing the educational experiences and outcomes of students of color.

1

Developing Racial Literacy and Cultural Awareness in Schools and Classrooms

TYRONE C. HOWARD

Race and culture in today's schools must be discussed. Educators at all levels need to develop the courage, knowledge, dispositions, and skills to understand the racial realities and cultural considerations brought about by demographic changes in US schools. In this chapter, I assert that critical wellness and social-emotional learning rely on educators' recognizing, understanding, and affirming students' racial and cultural identities. This chapter has three primary goals:

- Identify the changing racial demographics of today's schools and classrooms
- Discuss how and why race and culture matter in more diverse learning settings
- Offer strategies and resources for educators to strengthen their knowledge, skills, and dispositions to effectively teach across racial and cultural lines

There are many benefits to creating culturally supportive and affirming learning spaces. Developing racial literacy and cultural awareness nurtures more authentic teacher–student relationships. These, in turn, create greater trust and a stronger sense of psychological safety in the classroom. Supporting diverse learning environments helps educators improve curriculum design and delivery, as well as better understand the broader community being served. Most important, however, creating schools that are inclusive of students' identities, backgrounds, and realities is simply the right thing to do. Caring, democratic classrooms play a significant role in closing racial disparities in learning outcomes and in providing more and greater opportunities for individual students to thrive.[1]

Changing Nation, Changing Schools

Today's schools continue to change in new, unprecedented ways. One of the most pronounced changes has been in the ethnic, racial, cultural, and linguistic composition of today's students. These shifts in demographics have occurred rapidly—and continue at a remarkable pace in many cities, counties, and states across the country.

To better understand the changes we are seeing in today's student population, consider that the National Center for Education Statistics reports that Latinx youth will account for close to 30 percent of all students in the 2025 academic year. [2] The White student population is expected to drop precipitously from the 2003 level of 59 percent to approximately 46 percent by 2025. African American enrollment in public schools will remain constant over the next several decades, at approximately 15 percent, and the Asian American/Pacific Islander population will remain at approximately 6 percent over the next several years. Native American students will be approximately 1 percent of the school population in 2025, and the mixed-race population of students, which continues to increase, will be close to 4.5 percent. These numbers provide us a national snapshot, but a closer look at different metropolitan areas across the nation reveals some telling racial realities. Table 1.1 shows the fifteen largest school districts in the nation and the percentages of their non-White populations.

A broader examination of diversity in districts across the nation reveals that students of color represent a majority of the student body in 83 of the 100 largest cities. In all but three of those cities (Honolulu, Hawai'i, and Chula Vista and Fremont, California), at least half of students attend a school where a majority of their peers are poor or come from economically disadvantaged backgrounds. So as our schools are becoming increasingly diverse, the economic and racial segregation of these schools is important to note.[3] In addition to race and culture, the intersection with poverty also merits further examination.[4]

It is a mistake, however, to believe that these demographic changes are happening only in urban areas. The types of racial, ethnic, and cultural changes seen in large cities such as Los Angeles, New York, Houston,

TABLE 1.1 Largest School Districts in the United States

Rank	School District Name	Location	Enrollment	Non-White Population (%)
1	New York City Department of Education	New York	995,336	84.5
2	Los Angeles Unified School District	California	667,273	86
3	Puerto Rico Department of Education	Puerto Rico	437,202	100
4	Chicago Public Schools	Illinois	405,655	70
5	Miami-Dade County Public Schools	Florida	347,366	80
6	Clark County School District	Nevada	314,059	69
7	Broward County Public Schools	Florida	256,472	61
8	Houston Independent School District	Texas	204,245	82
9	Hillsborough County Public Schools	Florida	194,525	49
10	Hawaii Department of Education	Hawaii	179,601	88
11	Orange County Public Schools	Florida	176,008	58
12	School District of Palm Beach County	Florida	174,663	68
13	Fairfax County Public Schools	Virginia	174,479	60
14	School District of Philadelphia	Pennsylvania	166,233	71
15	Gwinnett County Public Schools	Georgia	160,744	75

Source: National Center for Education Statistics, Common Core of Data (CCD), "State Nonfiscal Public Elementary/ Secondary Education Survey Data, 2003–04 and 2013–14," https://nces.ed.gov/ccd/stnfis.asp.

and Chicago are now occurring in other communities across the nation.[5] States such as Ohio, Iowa, Minnesota, Nebraska, North and South Dakota, and Tennessee, to name just a few, are educating many more non-White students than they have in the past. Currently, fifteen states—Alaska, Arizona, California, Delaware, Florida, Georgia, Hawai'i, Louisiana, Maryland, Mississippi, Nevada, New Jersey, New Mexico, New York, and Texas—have more students of color than White students in their schools, with a number of other states expected to join them soon.[6]

And although a lot of attention has been given to large urban schools and the diversity they have experienced, it is also important to note that smaller cities and counties across the nation that were once racially homogenous are also witnessing increased racial and ethnic diversity. In many cases, suburban and rural schools now have "urban realities," meaning that the number of White students continues to decrease, and the number of non-White students continues to rise. Schools in Sioux Falls, South Dakota; Red Bank, New Jersey; Bloomington, Minnesota; and Gwinnett County, Georgia, have all transitioned from being majority White school districts to being majority non-White school districts.

In short, diversity is now a reality and the new normal in every state across the US. For many veteran teachers, this means that today's classrooms look dramatically different than the classrooms from the beginning of their teaching careers. This shift has many deep implications that reach well beyond changing complexions, languages, and identities in the classroom.

Race, Ethnicity, and Academic Outcomes

The persistent underachievement rates of students who come from racially and culturally diverse backgrounds is a critical issue in many schools and school districts wrestling with the rapid demographic transformation occurring in the United States.[7] This problem often affects African American, Native American, Latinx, and certain populations of Asian American students. Despite improvements in educational outcomes over the past several decades, these groups still lag behind their Asian American, White, and more affluent peers.

These disparities have often been referred to as the "academic achievement gap." A number of education researchers, however, have questioned this moniker. Instead, they have advocated for a deeper understanding of larger structural conditions that contribute to these disparities and for a wider use of terminology and strategies that speak more to opportunity than to achievement. Education scholar Gloria Ladson-Billings has argued that for many students of color, academic disparities are more reflective of an "education debt" steeped in historical, economic, sociopolitical, and moral gaps than they are of actual effort.[8] H. Richard Milner has written that the disparities are more about "opportunity gaps," which are tied to gaps in teacher quality, housing and food security, access to quality health care, access to safe neighborhoods, and a number of other key areas that are critical to educational success.[9] Educators must develop a healthy understanding of historical, political, and economic structures that have a profound impact on students' ability to learn. To do anything less is professionally irresponsible and unfair to students, and disrupts efforts for optimal student wellness.

Race and Why It Matters in Teaching and Learning

To help educators develop greater racial literacy and cultural competence, we need to define key terms and establish a vocabulary of important concepts that informs work in diverse schools. Many social and biological scientists agree that there is no real biological definition for race. In essence, **race** is an idea or concept that has been socially developed by people over time and that is largely determined by phenotype (observable characteristics, such as skin color) as well as facial features (e.g., nose, eye structure, hair texture). Even though it is little more than a social construct, race still matters in today's schools and society. Race matters because many people still attach hierarchical social value to people's skin color and physical features. In many ways, being White has always been the standard bearer or the norm in the racial hierarchy. According to Reni Eddo-Lodge:

> Neutral is white. The default is white. Because we are born into an already written script that tells us what to expect from strangers due to their skin color, accents and social status, the whole of humanity is coded as white.[10]

To be clear, it's not actually the skin color that matters; it is the baggage about skin color that we as humans carry that makes race so difficult to address.

What do the changes in today's schools mean for teachers? The first challenge is to recognize the racial and cultural mismatch in many, if not most, schools across the nation. Whereas we have witnessed unprecedented student diversity in our schools, the teaching population remains largely White and female. This means that the potential for racial and cultural mismatch between students and teachers remains high. There is increasing evidence which suggests that teacher–student racial match works for some students more than others. Gershenson and his colleagues discovered that

> assigning a black male to a black teacher in the third, fourth, or fifth grades significantly reduces the probability that he drops out of high school, particularly among the most economically disadvantaged black males. Exposure to at least one black teacher in grades 3–5 also increases the likelihood that persistently low-income students of both sexes aspire to attend a four-year college.[11]

But as Geneva Gay has explained, "similar ethnicity between students and teachers may be potentially beneficial, but it is not a guarantee of pedagogical effectiveness."[12] It's important for educators to realize that racial mismatch does not prohibit a strong connection to students. Teachers from backgrounds different from those of their students must be aware of racial and cultural differences, but it is even more important that they be mindful of the process of building relationships with students.[13] For example, it is vital to understand what Black teachers know and do to connect with Black students. The same can be said for Latinx teachers and students. These exchanges are likely to include nuanced forms of communication and identification that other teachers may not be aware of in their interactions with the specific population. Teachers and students may both operate from a prejudicial perspective about one another upon an initial meeting. From that point forward, however, race can become less of an issue, which can enhance a teacher's ability to connect with students and help them thrive in the classroom.

Steps that teachers can take to build authentic relationships with students can include, but are not limited to, the following:

- Getting to know students
- Asking about and learning about students' interests, families, and friends
- Learning about students' likes and dislikes
- Getting to know parents and caregivers
- Sharing of self

The truth is that teachers from any ethnic, cultural, or racial background can be successful with any classroom group when they possess—or have the skills to acquire—the knowledge, attitudes, dispositions, and beliefs necessary to meet the needs of their students.[14] But attaining this knowledge and expressing these beliefs are not always easy. Education scholars Kerri Ullucci and Dan Beatty have made the case that White teachers often struggle with thinking about issues tied to race, and in particular Whiteness. They have offered a framework on color blindness that is steeped in the tenets of color consciousness, which suggests that White teachers should consider and question the ideas of individualism, meritocracy, Whiteness, and neutrality.[15] These authors anchor the color-blindness framework on three key constructs:

- *Whiteness.* The concept or idea that White is normal and is the highest standard in the racial hierarchy, though not explicitly stated, is apparent in the stories, histories, and struggles that are most prevalent in school curricula. This also incorporates an anti-Blackness ideology which demonizes that which is furthest from White.
- *Merit.* This concept assumes that each person operates and achieves based on his or her own personal capacity. It incorporates the notion that the work put forth, the effort invested, explains why some groups and individuals do well and others do not. It does not consider historical factors or account for opportunities, advantages, and privileges to which some groups have access both historically and in the present.
- *Individualism.* This tenet proposes that each person is responsible for his or her outcomes. It is very much tied to merit, wherein group responsibility and accountability are not goals. Personal success and achievement are the goals. This belief operates from a survival-of-the-fittest approach that stresses singular pursuit and accomplishment.

Ullucci and Beatty report that such a framework is desperately needed with White preservice teachers:

> Students [with White preservice teachers] frequently resist these lines of conversation, creating intellectual roadblocks that in a domino-like way stymie further talk about culturally relevant teaching, critical pedagogy, and equitable schooling in general. When students enact a color-blind perspective, it automatically challenges the legitimacy of our work. Why do [these] students need a course on race and education if they have decided race plays *no role in education?*[16]

Similarly, colleague H. Richard Milner and I contend that racial and cultural knowledge should be just as important an element of teacher education as subject matter and pedagogical content knowledge. In the *Handbook of Urban Education*, we state:

> Because White teachers and students of color, in ways, possess different racialized and cultural experiences and repertoires of knowledge and knowing, both inside and outside the classroom, racial and cultural incongruence may serve as a roadblock for academic and social success in the classroom.[17]

Issues tied to race, ethnicity, and Whiteness can be complicated for many educators, but the demographics of today's students make it imperative that all educators remain mindful of who they are and whom they're teaching. Questions that teachers should consider as they seek to be more racially aware include the following:

- What are the racial demographics in my school?
- What are the racial demographics in my classroom?
- What are the racial demographics in my school's community?
- How have the racial demographics changed since I have been at my school?
- How much has my curriculum (content) changed to reflect the makeup of my students?
- Do I incorporate content that reflects racial and ethnic diversity?
- Do I feel comfortable responding to issues around race in the classroom?

There are any number of resources out there for further reading on the subject of race, some of which I have included at the end of the chapter.

Discomfort in Talking about Race

For many people in the United States, race has always been one of the most difficult topics to discuss. Issues around race and racism are often challenging to consider because of the nation's ugly past with regard to race. Slavery, colonization, segregation, Jim Crow laws, anti-Semitism, and a history of hate groups have always made race a polarizing topic. In addition, today's political climate has intensified many of our fears around race. Topics such as immigration, Black Lives Matter, nativism, nationalism, and xenophobia continue to create awkwardness and divisiveness around racial difference.

No other place demonstrates why we must come to grips with our racial realities more than our schools. Unfortunately, racism persists as a component of the educational climate in today's schools. The differing experiences that students encounter across racial lines have a profound influence on academic outcomes. To help all students thrive and achieve optimal levels of wellness, every student's identity, ethnicity, and cultural practices must be recognized and affirmed. One of the mistakes that many teachers make when it comes to race is to adopt a so-called color-blind approach. Although this may sound like an egalitarian strategy, it creates a number of problems. In an attempt to avoid racial awkwardness, many well-meaning teachers say things such as

- I was taught to see all people as the same.
- I was taught to see people, not color.
- I don't even notice my students' skin color.
- Talking about race only leads to racism.
- Racism doesn't exist anymore, so why bring it up?

This approach is problematic because it denies students' racial identities. Identities are an essential part of who each and every one of us is as a human. All individuals maintain multiple identities, related to such elements as race, gender identity, language, family position, and sexual orientation. To state that we do not see or acknowledge some aspects of students' identities is to deny significant parts of who they are, what some students may see as an important part of how they see themselves and how the world sees them. So teachers must develop comfort with dismantling color-blind approaches. In many ways, color-blind approaches can communicate to students that their race and ethnicity are not important or that their race and ethnicity are invisible. An important step that teachers can take is to incorporate content, children's literature, readings, novels, and examples that are told by and about people of color. Today there are a host of recommended works that teachers can consider on this topic. To learn more about these resources, see the recommended resources section at the end of the chapter.

In an attempt to be responsive to and mindful of the racial demographics of the classroom, it is important for teachers to

- Acknowledge the racial demographics
- Pay attention to those students who are part of the racial minority
- Develop racial literacy that enables discussions or topics tied to race and racism to be an integral part of the classroom

To tap into racial realities, teachers must recognize the importance of race, understand its impact on learning, and listen to the stories, experiences, concerns, and fears that students of color may share about their experiences as racialized beings.

Understanding Culture

For teachers to be able to connect with today's learners, they need to understand the important role that culture plays in all of our lives. At the core, we are all cultural beings. US society places an inordinate amount of focus and attention on race, but fundamentally it is culture that makes us who we are as groups and individuals. To know people is to know culture.[18] To understand people is to understand their cultural ways of being, knowing, communicating, and participating in the world. And, most important, to enhance learning opportunities for culturally diverse students, we must enable students to maintain cultural integrity in schools and classrooms, and enable students' cultural capital to be a conduit to learning.[19]

What we know about culture is that it shapes our ways of being, thinking, acting, communicating, and interpreting the world around us. Social scientists have not agreed on a definition of *culture* as a term. The general consensus is that **culture** is the way of life for a particular social group. Multicultural education scholar James Banks, who is considered a pioneer on the topic of culture and education, contends that "cultures are dynamic, complex, and changing."[20] In essence, culture is not static; people's ways of understanding the world are always changing, always evolving based on new situations, circumstances, and environmental factors.

Culture is generally taken to be a positive term. If there is anything people do naturally, it is that they live culturally, in groups, with goals, rules, expectations, customs, celebrations, abstractions, norms, dos and don'ts, and a litany of untold complexities. Culture gives us all we know and the tools with which to learn more. When anthropologists talk about the coherence of culture, there is an implication that all the people in the culture are the same. It can be a huge mistake, however, to assume that this is true.

To be clear, culture exists within and across groups. Although there are particular aspects of culture that are common in individual ethnic groups, that does not mean that all members of a racial group operate under the same cultural norms and ways of knowing and being. To the contrary—and this is very important for educators to note—individuals can be from different racial backgrounds and have more in common culturally than some members who are racially similar. To this end, teachers who are from different racial backgrounds than their students must avoid believing that they cannot connect with students because they are not from the same ethnic or racial group. When culture is understood as the knowledge that people need for living with each other, it is easy to focus on how some people appear to have more cultural knowledge than others just based on physical traits. This thinking must be rejected. For all teachers, no matter their race or ethnicity, it is important to develop a healthy sense of cultural awareness and competence across the full spectrum of backgrounds.

In responding to the needs of today's diverse learners, educators must enhance their competency when it comes to culture. Cultural competence cannot be taught in a superficial way that reduces culture to simplistic norms or expectations. There must be an understanding that culture is a complex phenomenon deeply embedded in behaviors, tools, practices, and ways of knowing, communicating, and surviving in a given context—and that these behaviors and practices are not bound by racial group classification. Culture is messy and contradictory at times. It is fluid, taking new shapes and forms across space, time, and generation with different social groups.[21]

Education scholar Geneva Gay says, "The cultural divide between White teachers and communities of color are [*sic*] often quite vast and to expect new teachers to bridge that divide without support may be unrealistic."[22] Nevertheless, it is a gap that must be bridged if teachers of diverse students are to succeed in authentically practicing cultural relevance in their work with students, families, and communities. In sum, culture and race are two different concepts, with different meanings and different ways in which they manifest. Race is seen more as a social construct, understood best by phenotype and other physical characteristics (eyes, nose, and hair). By contrast, culture is the compilation of ways of knowing, doing, being, and thinking, in addition to values, norms, and ways of living that are typically learned in response to a given environment. To be clear, there can be significant overlap between race and culture, but they are not always perfectly aligned.

Current teacher and student demographics can lead to a significant cultural knowledge gap between teachers and students, which Gay and Howard refer to as the *demographic divide.*[23] Therefore, any attempt to prepare a largely White teacher population to teach an increasingly non-White student population must be enacted on a larger scale in US schools. Doing so is contingent on helping teachers bridge the cultural knowledge gap so common in many classrooms.[24] What is needed is a way not only to translate theory to practice for teachers but also to be clearer about the development of cultural competence for all classroom teachers. Cultural competence cannot be developed in a superficial way that presents it only as an appreciation of foods, holidays, and festivals.

To deepen learning and understanding, additional resources on the various dimensions of culture are included at the end of the chapter.

First, though, take a moment to reflect on a few scenarios that mirror the experience of teaching in a diverse classroom.

What Would You Do?

To gain clarity into some of the challenges related to how race and culture can play out in classroom settings, consider the following scenarios for thought and discussion.

Scenario 1: You teach first grade at a predominantly African American school. At the end of recess, you are talking with one of your first-grade colleagues, who is a White woman. You are discussing your plans for the weekend, when you both realize that you need to retrieve your students and get them back to class. As you are finishing your sentence, your colleague, enthralled by the conversation says, "OK, OK, OK, I gotta go and get my little monkeys and get them back in class. Let's finish talking at lunch!"

Questions

1. Would this comment give you pause? Why or why not?
2. Would you say something to your colleague? If so, what?
3. What if your colleague says that you blew her comment way out of proportion and are just being sensitive. What would you say?

Scenario 2: Mr. Lord is a nice guy who has just been hired at your school to teach algebra. You notice quickly that Lord seems to have a quick trigger and little patience, and repeatedly sends students to the office for disciplinary issues. You notice that in this racially mixed school, almost all of the students Lord sends to the office for behavior problems are African American students. Several of the African American students tell you that Lord "doesn't like Black people" and that they don't want to be in his class.

Questions

1. How would you approach Mr. Lord on this issue?
2. How would you respond if he rejects the students' claims?
3. What would you do if, after the talk, the same pattern continues?

Scenario 3: Your colleague is talking to you about the students in your department. She mentions that it is becoming increasingly difficult to serve some of the students "because of their backgrounds." You are not quite sure what she means by this, but as she proceeds she mentions that "some of the Asians need to learn better English." Later in the conversation, she also talks about how she thinks that "a lot of the Hispanic students are illegal aliens, and maybe they should be reported." By all accounts your coworker is a very sweet person whom you've really liked for a long time.

Questions

1. What, if anything, would you say to your coworker who is making these comments?
2. What are the downsides of not saying anything?
3. What are the downsides of saying something?
4. Would you confide in another coworker?

KEY TAKEAWAYS

- Racial and ethnic diversity is here to stay in our country. Cities, states, counties, districts, and parishes across the country must embrace our "new normal" of increasingly non-White student populations in our schools. Therefore, school personnel must develop the knowledge, skills, dispositions, and competencies to teach, talk, and learn across racial, ethnic, cultural, and linguistic backgrounds.
- Issues tied to race and culture are frequently misunderstood, dismissed, or outright ignored. School personnel cannot diminish core aspects of students' identities. Racial realities in today's schools require teachers and staff to eliminate color-blind mentalities, understand the history of race and racism in the United States, and understand how racial disparities continue to exist in schools today.
- The incorporation of ethnic and racial content in the classroom is important to help students engage in learning. Moreover, curricula reflective of today's student populations can lead to better academic experiences and outcomes for some of today's most marginalized students.

Questions from the Field

In our conversations with teachers, very important questions regarding race and culture arise. The following are a few that I hope are helpful in your work with students.

1. *How can I be mindful of culture when I have students from many different cultures in my classroom?*
   The key is to talk to students. Observe students. Get to know students. Do not make assumptions about students based on skin color, last name, or appearance. If you take note of what students write about and talk about, you can learn who students are culturally.

2. *How can I talk about race if I am really uncomfortable discussing such a topic?*
   Begin to learn more about race. Read about race and racism. Talk with people across the racial spectrum about their stories, struggles, and experiences. Acknowledge your lack of knowledge, and take steps to learn more, do more, and see racially diverse students as potential sources of information.

3. *If I teach in a racially homogeneous classroom, there is really no need to talk about race, correct?*
   No, this is not correct! Racially homogeneous classrooms, though decreasing in numbers, need more access to racial and cultural diversity than racially heterogeneous classrooms. Lack of exposure to racial, ethnic, and cultural diversity can lead students to reify negative stereotypes and prejudice about certain groups. Help students broaden their scope through literature, novels, and current events about diverse populations.

4. *Doesn't talking more about race only lead to racism?*
   No. Avoiding race-related conversations can send the message to students that this is a taboo topic that is not to be discussed. This can lead to normalizing Whiteness and not understanding the histories, struggles, and accomplishments of racially diverse groups. Talking about race-related topics is key to reducing prejudice and dismantling stereotypes.

5. *Where can I learn more about topics related to race and culture?*
   See the recommended resources in the following section.

Recommended Resources

Tatum, B. D. (1997/2017). *Why are all the black kids sitting together in the cafeteria?* New York, NY: Basic Books. The premise of this book is that adults, both White and of color, often hesitate to speak to children about racism for fear they will create problems where perhaps none exist, afraid that they will make "color-blind" children unnecessarily color conscious.

Tatum responds to these issues and others, bringing useful clarity to the daily discourse about race.

Bonilla-Silva, E. (2003). *Racism without racists: Color-blind racism and the persistence of racial inequality in America.* **Lanham, MD: Rowman & Littlefield.** This book documents how, beneath our contemporary conversation about race, there lies a full-blown arsenal of arguments, phrases, and stories that many Whites use to account for—and ultimately justify—racial inequalities. The fifth edition of this provocative book makes clear that color-blind racism is as insidious now as ever. It features new material on our current racial climate, including the Black Lives Matter movement; a significantly revised chapter that examines the Obama presidency, the 2016 election, and Trump's presidency; and a new chapter addressing what readers can do to confront racism—both personally and on a larger, structural level.

Howard, T. C. (2010). *Why race and culture matter in schools.* **New York, NY: Teachers College Press.** Although race and culture remain important variables in how young people experience schools, they are often misunderstood by educators and school personnel. Building on three studies that investigated schools that were successful in closing the achievement gap, I show how adopting greater awareness and comprehensive understanding of race and culture can improve educational outcomes.

Milner, H. R., IV. (2015). *Rac(e)ing to class.* **Cambridge, MA: Harvard Education Press.** In this incisive and practical book, H. Richard Milner IV provides educators with a crucial understanding of how to teach students of color who live in poverty. Milner looks carefully at the circumstances of these students' lives and describes how those circumstances profoundly affect their experiences within schools and classrooms. In a series of detailed chapters, Milner proposes effective practices—at the district and school levels and in individual classrooms—for school leaders and teachers who are committed to creating the best educational opportunities for these students.

DiAngelo, R. (2018). *White fragility: Why it's so hard for white people to talk about racism.* **Boston, MA: Beacon Press.** In this book, Robin DiAngelo explains how White people misunderstand the concept of racism and therefore refuse to talk about it openly. She uses her experience as a diversity trainer to explain how America is inherently racist and that all White people must be courageous enough to see their complicity in the racist system. *White Fragility* digs deep into White culture and history to reveal some hidden facets of White society that many wouldn't openly expose. DiAngelo's goal is to show White people how racism works at an individual level so that they can understand just how damaging it is to society as a whole—and, she hopes, so they can fix it.

Morris, M. W. (2015). *Pushout: The criminalization of black girls in schools.* **New York, NY: New Press.** Morris looks at the lives of Black girls who are faced with school-related arrest, to discover the deeper stories beneath the surface. The results are shocking. There are girls who are abused; trafficked for sex; harassed because of race, gender, sexual orientation, or a combination of all three; and/or otherwise violated. And yet, Morris writes, somehow in these girls' progress through the juvenile justice system, the crimes against them have not come to light.

Sensoy, O., & DiAngelo, R. (2017). *Is everyone really equal?* **(2nd ed.). New York, NY: Teachers College Press.** This practical book will introduce readers to key concepts around social justice education, providing tools for developing "critical social justice literacy" and for taking action toward a more just society. Accessible to students from high school through graduate school and beyond, this book offers a collection of detailed and engaging explanations of key concepts in social justice education, including critical thinking, socialization, group identity, prejudice, discrimination, oppression, power, privilege, and White supremacy. Drawing on their extensive experience in a range of settings in the United States and Canada, the authors address the most common stumbling blocks to understanding social justice. They provide recognizable examples, scenarios, and vignettes illustrating these concepts.

Stevenson, H. C. (2014). *Promoting racial literacy in schools: Differences that make a difference.* **New York, NY: Teachers College Press.** Based on extensive research, this provocative volume explores how schools are places where racial conflicts often remain hidden, at the expense of a healthy school climate and the well-being of students of color. Most schools fail to act on racial microaggressions because the stress of negotiating such conflicts is extremely high due to fears of incompetence, public exposure, and accusation. Instead of facing these conflicts head on, schools perpetuate a set of avoidance or coping strategies. Stevenson uncovers how racial stress undermines student achievement. Students, educators, and social service support staff will find workable strategies to improve their racial literacy skills, enabling them to read, recast, and resolve racially stressful encounters when they happen.

Winn, M. T. (2018). *Justice on both sides.* **Cambridge, MA: Harvard Education Press.** Restorative justice represents "a paradigm shift in the way Americans conceptualize and administer punishment," says author Maisha T. Winn, from a focus on crime to a focus on harm, including the needs of both those who were harmed and those who caused it. This book provides a comprehensive account of the value of restorative justice and how contemporary schools can implement effective practices to address inequalities associated with race, class, and gender.

Love, B. (2019). *We want to do more than survive.* **Boston, MA: Beacon Press.** Drawing on her life's work of teaching and researching in urban schools, Bettina Love argues that educators must teach students about racial violence, oppression, and how to make sustainable change in their communities through radical civic initiatives and movements. She argues that the US educational system is maintained by and profits from the suffering of children of color. Instead of trying to repair a flawed system, education reformers offer survival tactics in the forms of test-taking skills, acronyms, grit labs, and character education, which Love calls the educational survival complex.

2

How to Create a Trauma-Aware Learning Environment

MAISAH HOWARD

As educators and individuals charged with ensuring that all children have an opportunity to reach their full academic potential, we must understand trauma and the impact it has on learning, social emotional health, and critical wellness. Most educators won't hear detailed accounts of a student's trauma. It's likely that this information may never be known by the myriad teachers or other school officials whom a child encounters. After reading this chapter, you'll be able to recognize the symptoms of trauma without needing to know a child's story. As you begin to recognize the symptoms of trauma, you can respond in a manner that supports healing.

To better understand the symptoms and implications of trauma, consider the case of a student we'll call Tasha. In class, Tasha appears disruptive. Almost every day that she comes to class, she talks a lot and disrupts learning for others. Teachers often try to redirect her. She's sassy, however, and mouths off to her teachers in front of the class, often causing the class to erupt in laughter. She frequently skips full days of school, or simply shows up for a few classes. When a teacher sends a warning note home to be signed by a parent, Tasha forges the signature and returns the note. When teachers tell Tasha that they'll call her mother, she acts indifferent. But whenever possible, Tasha intercepts these calls. And despite all of her poor behavior and frequent absences, Tasha is bright and performs well academically.

Although it may appear that Tasha is causing major disruptions in school, the reality is that she's experiencing extreme adversity. Tasha's father has been incarcerated for all but six months of her life, and she's being raised by her single mother in an underresourced and underserved community.

When Tasha was just six years old, her father escaped from prison. In response, FBI and local law enforcement officials raided the home she shared with her mom and siblings. During the raid, they were all paraded outside, where neighbors and other passersby could see her family on public display. Tasha returned to school the next day, but it was extremely difficult for her to concentrate on learning when she had just experienced such a terrifying event.

Tasha is impacted not only by having a father in prison but also by her mother's physical and emotional abuse. As a method of discipline Tasha's mother requires her to disrobe and then beats her with extension cords, belts, or other objects. Because of this abuse, Tasha has sustained welts, bruises, and open wounds on her body. Tasha dresses in a manner that hides her wound, and she frequently opts not to dress for gym because of her visible injuries. Sometimes Tasha's mother burns her fingertips on the stove as a form of punishment.

Although Tasha is able to conceal these physical wounds, she's never asymptomatic of the trauma she's experiencing—and it clearly impacts her in school. Whenever the school calls home to report Tasha's behavior, her mother punishes her with food deprivation, not permitting her to eat dinner with the family. Over time, Tasha has learned to anticipate all the various forms of discipline. To counter the food deprivation, she often takes food from school for later consumption. Even with her disruptive behavior, Tasha has never been identified as an abused or neglected child by a child welfare agency, and school personnel have never been alerted to her many traumatic experiences.

Educators need to understand that an abusive parent or adult caregiver may not look or act like an abuser. Tasha's mom is an active participant in her child's education. She's what many educators would call an engaged parent. She attends back-to-school nights, open houses, parent-teacher conferences, and Parent Teacher Association meetings, yet she's abusive to Tasha.

As educators, we need to acknowledge that we don't know what we don't know. And we certainly don't know what happens behind closed doors in students' homes. Unfortunately, there are countless "Tashas" in schools and classrooms across this country. Their stories vary, as does the impact of their traumas, but their ability to remain resilient is often predicated on their access to loving, supportive adults who can serve as a buffer in the midst of their storm.

As individuals charged with ensuring that all children have an opportunity to reach their full academic potential, we must understand trauma and the impact it has on learning, social emotional health, and critical wellness. Moreover, we must acknowledge that not all children come to school with the same access to opportunities, support systems, and structures needed to thrive. To help promote increased classroom equity, this chapter will start by defining trauma and explaining a well-known framework for understanding its prevalence and its impact on critical wellness. Next, I'll provide best practices for caring for and serving students who have experienced trauma. This includes ways to identify and respond to distressed students, empower and collaborate with them, and limit your own judgment.

What Is Trauma?

To truly understand childhood trauma, it's imperative that we first have a working definition of **trauma**. According to the Department of Health and Human Services, Children's Bureau, "Trauma is an emotional response to an intense event that threatens or causes harm. The harm can be physical or emotional, real or perceived, and it can threaten the child or someone close to him or her. Trauma can be the result of a single event, or it can result from exposure to multiple events over time."[1]

There are various types of trauma, and it's essential for educators to become familiar with some of them. For instance, students can experience acute, chronic, complex, historical, and intergenerational trauma. The following are definitions of each:

- **Acute trauma** is a single-incident trauma.[2]
- **Chronic trauma** is exposure to recurrent and prolonged traumatic events.[3]
- **Complex trauma** comprises traumatic experiences that are severe and pervasive. According to the National Child Traumatic Stress Network, "These traumas include exposure to different and numerous traumatic occurrences. Complex trauma generally begins early in childhood, and has the ability to interrupt various parts of a child's development, and can impede a child's ability to form healthy attachment bonds with others."[4]

- **Historical trauma** is the collective and cumulative emotional and psychological wounding over the life span and across generations, emanating from massive group trauma experiences.[5]
- **Intergenerational trauma** comprises the trauma experiences transmitted across generations, affecting the children, grandchildren, and other offspring of those who were initially victimized.[6]

Childhood trauma is real and pervasive. An examination of childhood trauma statistics reveals the following:

- Of the nearly seventy-six million youth living in the United States, about forty-six million are trauma survivors.[7]
- One study of children ages two to five found that 52 percent had experienced a severe stressor in their lifetime.[8]
- One out of every four children attending school has been exposed to a traumatic event that can affect learning or behavior.[9]
- A report of child abuse is made every ten seconds.[10]
- Suicide is the third leading cause of death among children ages ten to fourteen.[11]
- Teenagers are three times more likely than younger children to suffer multiple victimizations by multiple perpetrators.[12]

These statistics illustrate the prevalence of childhood trauma. The research tells us that childhood trauma affects brain structure and function, learning, cognitive development, social-emotional development, behavior, and physical well-being.[13] Clearly, childhood traumas have a tremendous impact on lifelong health, wellness, opportunity, and success. In light of this, these early experiences are an important educational issue. Much of the foundational research in this area has revolved around what's come to be known as adverse childhood experiences (ACEs).

Adverse Childhood Experiences (ACEs)

In the late 1990s, Dr. Vincent Felitti at Kaiser Permanente in San Diego, California, and Dr. Robert Anda with the Centers for Disease Control and Prevention examined the impact of **adverse childhood experiences** (ACEs) on adult physical and mental well-being.[14] This research has profound implications for understanding how trauma impacts children over a lifetime. ACEs are experiences from childhood ages zero to eighteen that involve physical, emotional, or sexual abuse; physical or emotional neglect; parental mental illness; substance dependence; parental incarceration; parental separation or divorce; and parental domestic violence. The original ACE questionnaire has ten questions, as shown here. A yes response to any question yields 1 point, for a possible total score of 10.

Adverse Childhood Experience (ACE) Questionnaire

FINDING YOUR ACE SCORE

While you were growing up, during your first 18 years of life:

1. Did a parent or other adult in the household **often** . . .
   Swear at you, insult you, put you down, or humiliate you?
   or
   Act in a way that made you afraid that you might be physically hurt?

   Yes   No   If yes enter 1 _____

2. Did a parent or other adult in the household **often** . . .
   Push, grab, slap, or throw something at you?
   or
   Ever hit you so hard that you had marks or were injured?

   Yes   No   If yes enter 1 _____

3. Did an adult or person at least 5 years older than you **ever** . . .
   Touch or fondle you or have you touch their body in a sexual way?
   or
   Try to or actually have oral, anal, or vaginal sex with you?

   Yes   No   If yes enter 1 _____

4. Did you **often** feel that . . .
   No one in your family loved you or thought you were important or special?
   or
   Your family didn't look out for each other, feel close to each other, or support each other?

   Yes   No   If yes enter 1 _____

5. Did you **often** feel that . . .

   You didn't have enough to eat, had to wear dirty clothes, and had no one to protect you?

   > **or**

   Your parents were too drunk or high to take care of you or take you to the doctor if you needed it?

   > Yes   No   If yes enter 1 _____

6. Were your parents **ever** separated or divorced?

   > Yes   No   If yes enter 1 _____

7. Was your mother or stepmother:

   Often pushed, grabbed, slapped, or had something thrown at her?

   > **or**

   Sometimes or often kicked, bitten, hit with a fist, or hit with something hard?

   > **or**

   Ever repeatedly hit over at least a few minutes or threatened with a gun or knife?

   > Yes   No   If yes enter 1 _____

8. Did you live with anyone who was a problem drinker or alcoholic or who used street drugs?

   > Yes   No   If yes enter 1 _____

9. Was a household member depressed or mentally ill or did a household member attempt suicide?

   > Yes   No   If yes enter 1 _____

10. Did a household member go to prison?

   > Yes   No   If yes enter 1 _____

Now add up your Yes answers: _____ This is your ACE score.

Source: Adverse Childhood Experiences Questionnaire. (2019). Traumadissociation.com. Retrieved May 22, 2019, from http://traumadissociation.com/ace. Try it yourself: http://traumadissociation.com/ace.

The ACE study had 17,421 adult participants. The study sample was 70 percent White and 70 percent college educated. The study shed light on just how common ACEs are for individuals. Of the participants in the original ACE study, 67 percent had an ACE score of at least 1, and 12.6 percent had an ACE score of 4 or greater.[15] The reality is that many of the students and families being served in US public schools across the country do not reflect the demographic in the original ACE study and face a multitude of adverse experiences that are not even indicated on the ACE instrument. In 2015, traditional public schools in the United States were 49 percent White, 15 percent Black, 26 percent Hispanic, 5 percent Asian, 1 percent American Indian/Alaskan Native, and 3 percent two or more races.[16] A different study, the Philadelphia Urban ACE Survey, was conducted in 2013. This study was intended to address the impact of childhood adversities facing young people in urban communities that were not considered or addressed in the original ACE study. The study discovered just how pervasive ACEs were for youth in underserved, marginalized communities.[17]

ACEs and Children in Schools

As mentioned, the students being served in US public schools across this nation in urban, rural, and suburban communities face a host of adversities that are not indicated on the original ACE instrument. Some students have lost parents, siblings, or other significant individuals in their lives. There are students living with family members who are battling chronic or terminal illnesses or who themselves are battling such illnesses. Other students are experiencing homelessness or transiency, or food or financial insecurity; some live in persistent poverty or in communities that regularly experience violence and high crime. There are students who are newcomers or refugees, and others who are concerned about their own or their family members' immigration status. Some students are bullied or victimized. A child experiencing any one of these factors can be adversely impacted. Consider the fact that there are students who arrive at schools each and every day who are experiencing two or more stressors simultaneously. How might those students present in school or in your classroom? Students often go into survival mode. While in survival mode students fight, freeze, or flee. When students go into survival mode they are often using the coping strategies that they have learned to cope with their stressors. Table 2.1 identifies how the "flight," "fight," and "freeze" reactions may reveal themselves.[18]

TABLE 2.1   How Students Who Experience Trauma May Present in the Classroom: Lessons from the ACE Study

Flight	Fight	Freeze
• Withdrawing	• Acting out	• Exhibiting numbness
• Fleeing the classroom	• Behaving aggressively	• Refusing to answer
• Skipping class	• Acting silly	• Refusing to get needs met
• Daydreaming	• Exhibiting defiance	
• Seeming to sleep	• Being hyperactive	• Giving a blank look
• Avoiding others	• Arguing	• Feeling unable to move or act
• Hiding or wandering	• Screaming/yelling	
• Becoming disengaged		

Although somewhat limited in scope, the ACE study served to demonstrate the powerful impact that early adversity has on children over a life span. The authors of the original ACE study found that traumas impacted the social and emotional well-being and physical health of adults who experienced severe stressors and traumatic experiences in their childhood. Researchers were able to correlate ACE scores with health outcomes. The research demonstrated that the higher the ACE score, the worse the health outcomes were over a lifetime.[19]

Individuals with an ACE score of 4 or greater were three-and-a-half times more likely to develop chronic obstructive pulmonary disease (COPD), twice as likely to develop heart disease and cancer, and four-and-a-half times more likely to suffer from depression relative to an individual with an ACE score of 0.[20] There are numerous other health markers as well. Individuals with an ACE score of 6 or greater on average had a twenty-year difference in life expectancy relative to individuals with an ACE score of 0.[21] Individuals with an ACE score of 4 or greater were seven times more likely to go to prison relative to an individual with an ACE score of 0.[22] Educators can serve as a buffer to disrupt some of these poor health and life trajectories.

A research study conducted in Spokane, Washington, discovered that elementary school students with high ACE scores demonstrated a higher incidence of absences, behavioral issues, difficulty in school, and health-related issues.[23] In fact, 51 percent of children with an ACE score of 4 or greater experienced difficulties with learning or behavior compared to just

3 percent for children with an ACE score of 0.[24] Many children who have experienced ACEs do not have the words to express what has happened to them, yet there is a clear history and emotion about the traumatic event or experience that is likely to be the origin of many of the child's behaviors. Children often lack the sophistication to associate their behaviors to a precipitating traumatic event, and it is likely that the educators who serve them in schools do not make the connections either. For educators to begin to make the connection that a child's behavior might be a response to a traumatic life event and not simply willful defiance, they must notice and observe students rather than judge them. "Teachers and school personnel in trauma sensitive schools are 'emotional detectives': rather than judging students they try to understand them and help correct cognitive distortions that inhibit self-regulation."[25]

Connecting Student Behavior to ACEs

There's a connection between ACEs and the ABCs of behavior: **a**ntecedent, **b**ehavior, and **c**onsequence. What was happening before the observed behavior occurred? Knowing this helps you become aware of potential triggers for a student. Being aware of a student's triggers and identifying patterns in a student's response to various stimuli, along with giving that child tools to aid in self-regulation, can help offset behaviors. Children can be triggered by a host of scary or frightening reminders of a traumatic event. These possible triggers may include, but are not limited to, transitions, elevated speaking tones, fussing, shouting or verbal spats, loud noises, an anniversary of a particular event, certain times of the day, large groups of people, being touched, or certain smells.

Although behavior can be a direct result of a reminder or trigger, educators often overlook the importance of understanding triggers that directly influence student behavior. Such behaviors may be disruptive or unacceptable for a school or classroom community; however, it is crucial to recognize that all behavior is functional and that a specific behavior is trying to convey a message. Children often have difficulties communicating what they might need at a given time when an intrusive thought enters their mind related to a particular traumatic event. Although children rarely understand that the trauma they experienced is impacting their behavior, it's important for educators working with children to understand this connection, as well as the possible "meanings" of withdrawn, disruptive, or challenging behavior. No child is inherently bad. The key is to remember that thoughts of a traumatic event(s) can lead to feelings about the event(s), which in turn lead to behaviors or actions. Children do not always make the connection; however, educators should understand that trauma impacts both learning and behavior. The intrusive thoughts that children have about traumatic events or stressors activate internal responses. The amygdala sounds the alarm that there's a frightening event occurring. The amygdala tells the prefrontal cortex to shut down so that the body can react in order to survive (the fight-or-flight reaction previously illustrated in Table 2.1). The hippocampus records this event so that the brain recognizes it when it happens again. When there is repeated exposure to trauma, the mere reminder (trigger) sets off the alarm and overrides the prefrontal cortex, the body responds with a fight-or-flight response, and the hippocampus has a decreased ability to inhibit reactions to stimuli.[26]

It can be a challenge working with students who have experienced trauma. The good news is that the brain is plastic. **Brain plasticity** refers to the brain's ability to change throughout the life span. The brain has the remarkable capacity to reorganize itself and establish new connections between brain cells.[27] There's hope that all students with proper support and nurturing have the ability to change. Students do not have to be defined by their traumatic experiences. Students who have experienced trauma "might be forever changed by their experiences, but they are surely not forever damaged."[28]

Individuals working with students who are currently experiencing or may have experienced trauma need to find ways to reduce, rather than contribute to, the trauma students are already suffering. To that end, it's important to discuss ways of caring for students who've experienced trauma. Many of the practices adopted to care for students who have experienced trauma can also be generalized practices that benefit all students. The next section outlines a number of considerations and best practices for supplying this type of support to students who have experienced trauma.

Trauma-Informed Care

Trauma-informed care involves an acknowledgment of the pervasiveness of trauma, knowledge and understanding of how trauma affects the students that you serve, and a response that aids students in feeling physically and emotionally safe. In trauma-informed care it is important to connect the presenting behavior in context considering the whole child and his or her possible trauma history. Trauma-informed care supports healing and does no harm. In caring for students with a history of trauma, it's critical to provide trauma-informed care. As discussed in the previous section, the first step in doing so is recognizing that all behavior is functional. This is so important, it is worth repeating: children often try to communicate through their play and behavior what they may not be able to convey through language. When educators fail to provide trauma-informed care, they often label a student's behavior as "bad." That said, as author and youth advocate Father Greg Boyle explained, "bad behavior should be recognized as the language that it is: the vocabulary of the deeply wounded."[29]

Practitioners should work in tandem with their students identifying ways to collaborate and offer students choices. By providing students with choices educators empower their students. Traditional practices of school discipline seek rudimentary compliance and obedience, with little flexibility. Often children who have experienced trauma are seeking safety, empowerment, and choice. Many of these children had little or no control over the events they endured. Typically, someone or something exerted power over them. Therefore, it's important for students to be empowered. Students need to be given opportunities to make choices. They need to have their voices heard and, more important, acknowledged. We should listen to students as passionately as we want to be heard by them. Empowerment occurs when teachers work in tandem with students to help them achieve optimal success. To help cultivate this sort of environment, try to avoid hierarchical relationships in the classroom. Students who have experienced trauma will often reject a hierarchical classroom management style. For many students, this style represents yet another way for someone—in this case, the educator—to leverage power and control over them.

Some students may experience home circumstances that leave them in a **parentified** position. This means that a child has assumed a parental role within the household unit. When a child assumes this role, it can be difficult for that child to shift from her or his role as the responsible "parent" at home to the compliant student in the classroom and at school. Be aware of your students' realities and consider those realities when working with them, to better understand what their behavior is communicating.

Some educators do harm to children merely by how they choose to manage or "control" their classrooms. Educators often associate classroom management with managing students' behaviors in the classroom. I challenge educators to shift their mindset about what classroom management truly means. Authors Gianna Cassetta and Brook Sawyer appropriately describe classroom management as "being about building relationships with students and teaching social skills along with academic skills."[30] This approach to classroom management can significantly alter interactions between students and school personnel. A critical step toward providing this type of trauma-informed care is to learn to stop judging—something we all do, consciously or not—and to start noticing.

Stop Judging and Start Noticing

The truth is, most people are really good at judging. We all do it each and every day. It takes deliberate practice to simply observe or notice without judgment.

Students are often judged based on their appearance, behavior, academic achievement, and even family structure. Educators frequently label students' behaviors and learning styles in non-affirming terms, and children often internalize the "you talk" they hear about themselves. An educator might say, "You're always bad" or "You're always in trouble," or even, "You're not smart enough." These types of messages can have lasting effects. This "you talk" can become a child's "self-talk."[31] Children may begin to believe that they're the very things their teacher told them they were. "I am bad." "I am always in trouble." "I'm not smart enough."

Educator Becky Bailey asserts that students are often testing a hypothesis. "Am I really that unworthy, unlovable, and incapable of being successful?"[32] I believe that educators' daily responses to students both in the classroom and in school help inform children's answers to these type of questions and can ultimately impact students' beliefs about themselves. Educators and school personnel have the ability to help or hinder a child's academic and social emotional growth and development. To help, educators should refrain from judging students. Instead, they should start taking notice. When we observe, we simply identify what we see. If one truly observes and doesn't judge, there's no assigned value of right or wrong, of good or bad. There's mere reporting of what we see. When we judge, we place value on what we see, and infer information that was not provided.

FIGURE 2.1   What Do You Observe about This Young Man?

Consider in your practice and service to students whether you judge or observe them. One way that educators can observe as oppose to judge is to take note of students' behavior and be mindful of the language used to identify or characterize that behavior. Notice students' behavior and simply identify what is seen without any connotations or additional analysis. Then ask questions. Consider the young man in Figure 2.1.

The following are typical responses:

- He is sad.
- He has a headache.
- He is lonely.
- He is depressed.
- He has no friends.

These are all judgments. If we simply observe, our observations may include

- He has on jeans.
- He is wearing a white T-shirt.
- He has his hand on his head.
- He is wearing black shoes.

FIGURE 2.2   What Do You Observe about This Girl?

Instead of making assumptions, if we truly want to know what is going on with this child, we need to ask him. Now look at the girl in Figure 2.2. The following are typical responses:

- She is in a gang.
- She has money because she has jewelry.
- She is a chola.
- She doesn't go to school.

Again, these are all judgments. If we simply observe, our observations may include

- She has on earrings.
- She is wearing a necklace.
- She is wearing a tank top.
- She has an eyebrow piercing.
- She is leaning against a wall.

At times, we all feel upset or distressed. Sometimes we just have a bad day. This is true of students, too. When signs of struggle, challenge, and distress are present over time, however, it suggests that a student's problem could warrant more attention. Understanding—and practicing—the difference between observing a student versus judging a student is the first step in becoming sensitized to deeper problems and taking responsibility for the well-being of all students.

Identifying and Responding to Students in Distress

One of the questions educators frequently ask is, "How can I identify students who may be in distress?" To help identify troubled students, look for academic, safety risk, psychological, and or physical indicators.[33] As we practice observing, we can become attuned to students who may be experiencing stressors. Academic indicators could be decline in the overall quality of schoolwork, increased absences, or disconcerting content in the student's writing. Safety risk indicators could be threats to self or others. Behavioral indicators include unexplained rage, antagonism, or aggression. Psychological indicators include outward verbal assaults, extreme emotional responses, and self-disclosures. Physical indicators include excessive tiredness/sleepiness, transformations or alterations in appearance, and overall care of oneself.[34]

How might educators respond when recognizing a student who is experiencing distress? A teacher recently reported to me that a student fell asleep in the middle of an important quiz. Rather than responding in a manner that may have embarrassed the student or felt like chastising, the teacher simply walked over to the student and asked to speak with her outside. The teacher asked her if she was OK. The student initially giggled and said that she was fine. The teacher told her that he was concerned because she had fallen asleep during her quiz. The girl suddenly broke into a tearful outburst. The teacher asked her again if she was OK. The student then shared that her family was losing their home. The student explained that her parents had been fighting and that no one knew what would happen to them. The teacher allowed the student an opportunity to complete her quiz at a slightly later time more conducive to optimal performance. This particular teacher–student exchange is just one example of noticing and then responding in a manner that is helpful.

Remember—and I know I've reminded you of this a few times, but it's important—behavior is functional. Students' behavior is often being used to communicate a need. It's a way to convey to the adults in their lives that they need help, that they're hurting or suffering. Consider your response the next time you have a student who doesn't behave in a manner conducive to learning. Take notice—don't judge. When you notice, it can be OK to look and identify patterns. More often than not, however, it's more effective to notice and begin asking questions. You may point out to the student what you observed and then ask the student, "Is everything OK?" Then allow the student to choose whether or not to share or disclose any information with you. In the previous example, the student chose to share, but not all students will choose to do so. There are other approaches, too. Interactive journaling with students experiencing stressors is an alternative. Begin with a "free write" or some open-ended questions. You may also begin with writing prompts to get to know your students. As a start, consider the following:

- What do you wish your teacher knew about you?
- A day in the life of . . . (student's name).
- Just last week I . . . (fill in the blank with an achievement or activity).
- If someone wrote a book about your life, what would the title be?
- What is your greatest fear? Why?
- When are you happiest? Why?

At this point, it's critical to understand that childhood trauma or ACEs affect more than the students in a school or classroom. The reality is, childhood trauma—as studies have shown—influences sufferers long into adulthood. This means that educators themselves can be affected by stressors that occurred years or decades ago. Being sensitive to this reality has a direct effect on the relationships we as educators have with our students.

ACEs and Educators

As we've seen, educators need to understand how ACEs impact the lives of the students they serve; knowledge of ACEs also is useful in understanding and reflecting on how educators' own experiences of childhood adversity may impact and inform their practices. Teachers and other school personnel often come to school with their own histories of trauma. This history can positively or negatively influence the delivery of services. Some educators may assume that because they were able to demonstrate resilience and overcome their childhood adversities, so too should their students. But not all students have access to a healthy ecological system with parental supports, supportive relationships with teachers and other caring adults, adequate schools, community engagement, and well-resourced neighborhoods, all of which can serve as a buffer for those experiencing childhood adversity. Further, no two people who experienced the same, or similar, childhood adversities will respond to such stressors in the same way.

As educators recognize the impact of ACEs on adult social emotional well-being, whether in theory or in their own lives, I'm optimistic that they'll become more empathetic to students who demonstrate poor self-regulation. Some students who exhibit dysregulation are experiencing persistent adversity. In many ways, acknowledging past distress helps build, cultivate, and strengthen the educator's relationship with students.

Relationships Matter

I cannot stress enough the importance of relationships, of true connection. All students need at least one adult connection in the school—and it does not have to be with their teacher. It may be with a coach, cafeteria worker, school counselor, or someone else on the school staff. Find out who that adult is, and use the relationship that child has with that adult to bridge the gap in your own relationship with that child. Have that adult aid you in making a connection with that student. Educators also must acknowledge how they typically feel about a student, as that feeling is often reflected in the service delivery to that student. When educators are honest about how they feel about a particular student, then they have the ability to shift their thinking and overall disposition when working with that student. The ultimate litmus test for educators is whether they serve their students in a manner they would want an educator to serve their own child or family member. This is often easier said than done.

How should educators work to connect with a student who exhibits challenging behaviors, who is withdrawn, or who has some learning difficulties? Educators should seek ways to connect with the student by building rapport. This may be finding something that you both have in common and pointing it out. This can be as simple as recognizing that you both have the same hair color or same color pants or enjoy reading the same books. Find something that you both can share a smile or laugh about. Identify the strengths that this student possesses. Once those strengths are identified, the teacher must convey those strengths to that child. Some students have grown accustomed to hearing only the negative things that are said about them. Therefore, educators must share the student's strengths with the student—repeatedly. When possible, educators should try to identify the situations or contexts in which students are successful. When a teacher is able to identify these contexts, it then becomes possible to replicate those situations or circumstances to create success in other situations. When a student experiences difficulties or seems to struggle, teachers should consider what the student might need to be successful, and ask themselves what it is that they might do to help that student. Be prepared for the fact that the child may not have the language to articulate his or her needs. The following are some more practical strategies for ensuring critical wellness of traumatized students.

Practical Strategies for Working with Students

In trauma- or healing-responsive practice, educators need to create an affirming, safe, healthy, nurturing learning environment that encourages collaboration and bonding rather than hierarchical relationships. As I mentioned earlier in the chapter, students who have experienced toxic stress or trauma often have had no control over what happened to them, and frequently some adult has in some way leveraged power and/or control over them. Hierarchical relationships with these students are likely to cause undue stress between the student and the teacher. Students recognize that you are the teacher or individual responsible for their learning and safety while at school. It is not necessary to overtly demonstrate that through hierarchical exchanges.

Teachers should try to create a family-like classroom and school environment. Students spend an inordinate amount of time at school; some students spend more time with school personnel than they do with their families. The school community should demonstrate compassion and love, creating an environment where all children feel welcomed, valued, safe, and successful. As educators, we want to ensure that students know they matter. For effective learning to occur, students need to know that their academic, social, and emotional selves matter to those responsible for their learning. As the saying goes, "Students do not care what you know, until they know that you care."

When responding to a student's behavior, give yourself permission to pause and reflect before responding. Not all behavior requires an immediate response. Carefully consider the student's behavior and what that behavior may be trying to communicate. Take a moment to ask yourself, *Is this willful defiance?* Or, instead, could the behavior be a response to a traumatic life event or a call for help? Be mindful of the antecedent—what may have occurred prior to the presenting behavior or what trauma reminder might the child have experienced that may have evoked the response or behavior. Be curious, not judgmental. You may never know the specific stressors your students are experiencing, but you can still respond with healing approaches. You can respond to that child as you would any child who you know is in distress, without ever needing to know the specific circumstances that child finds himself or herself in. Choose to reduce—and not contribute to—the adversity and stressors that students experience.

Create a classroom environment that supports all facets of student growth. This means being flexible with your teaching methods by differentiating learning and assessments for some students. When examining equity and equality, you need to recognize that not all students have equal opportunities to be successful in school. To effectively serve the student populations in today's schools, educators must accept the fact that to achieve equity, some students require additional support. It's sometimes necessary to individualize instruction for students, and it's imperative that educators recognize that a win for each student looks different. Students should not be expected to all progress at the same level. Assist and guide students in setting goals, making choices, and engaging in self-reflection. Aid students in setting goals in a range where they will succeed, then continue to adjust the bar accordingly. Students need to experience some degree of success to believe in themselves, to maintain motivation, and to thrive.

Create status roles for students both within the classroom and in the school community. This means giving students who may not ordinarily be given an opportunity to lead a chance to demonstrate leadership and responsibility. This may include allowing students to serve as the line leader, paper monitor, peer helper, or student council representative. When students recognize that you trust them with responsibility, they often do not want to disappoint you. Give students a chance to feel important.

Responding to Challenging Students

Some students experience such strong, recurrent, and persistent adversity that toxic stress becomes their norm. Such severe and pervasive toxic stress should never be normal for anyone, yet it's a daily reality for some students. It's a privilege for educators and other adults to have the maturation and sophistication to process stressors. Most educators have recourse for the circumstances they endure. School staff can choose to call in sick, take leave, seek mental health services, or find numerous other ways to counter stressors. Children often do not have these same outlets. Educators must extend flexibility beyond the academic arena into disciplinary practices. Seek more restorative methods of disciplining students, rather than relying solely on punitive responses. Although it's important to hold students accountable for their actions with appropriate consequences, to cultivate critical wellness it's often necessary to rethink traditional discipline practices. Traditional disciplinary approaches typically focus on a violation of rules. Punitive responses to behavior usually rely on the ability of adults to leverage power over students.[35] Instead, we want to shift to a more restorative approach that focuses on a violation of people and relationships rather than rules. In restorative discipline practices, students are encouraged to problem-solve. They are given an opportunity to reflect on their actions and repair harm to relationships with peers or adults. Restorative approaches to discipline build healthy relationships between educators and students, while still holding students accountable. The following are a few quick tips for adopting an effective approach to school discipline:

Some Quick Tips for Working with Students Who Have Experienced Trauma

- Give students an opportunity to reflect on their undesirable behaviors. Have discussions about the behaviors and how the behaviors impacted others. Allow students an opportunity to repair the harm caused to relationships and people.
- Never publicly shame a student. Make every attempt to always address students' behaviors individually and not in the presence of an audience of their peers. In building rapport with students, the sacred act of not publicly shaming a student is colossal.
- Know your students and what they best respond to. Provide praise and encouragement for the behavioral and academic wins. Not all children,

however, want to receive public praise. When you know your students, you will know which students are accepting of public praise and which students prefer an individual acknowledgment.

- Identify the adult or adults on campus to whom a child is most connected. Solicit the support of those colleagues to encourage positive behavior and aid the child in self-regulation.
- Do not ever be so trauma aware that it impedes your ability to hold students accountable. Holding students accountable is another way that students assess that you care.

Reflection

In this chapter, I've shared information about the prevalence of ACEs. Now I encourage you to reflect for a moment on your current students and your own childhood experiences. Think about a time in your childhood when you might have experienced some type of adversity. Although it may be different than that of your students, the impact of the stressor may be similar. Ponder for a moment what an adult could have done to help you. What could a teacher have done to buffer your storm? This reflection is important as you develop practices to help students impacted by trauma.

Ensuring that all children have an opportunity to reach their full academic potential, while also tending to their social emotional health and wellness, can feel overwhelming. Educators should not need to serve as therapist for their students. Yet it's critical that all educators have an understanding of the impact that trauma has on learning, behavior, cognitive development, social emotional health, physical health, and overall well-being. This understanding should manifest itself as empathy, flexibility, and compassion.

Think about it this way: if you were asked to share your ACE score, it might feel a little bit uncomfortable. This may be because of guilt for having an ACE score of 0. Or maybe it would be because your ACE score is higher than you expected—and you know the painful story behind that score. In this case, your story may be painful to recall, and especially painful to share. You probably wouldn't voluntarily share it with people around you.

Why am I bringing this up? It's a simple reminder that you shouldn't expect to know the story to recognize the symptoms and harm that may have been caused by traumatic events. Those traumatic events lead to intrusive thoughts of the events, which, in turn, lead to feelings about the event. And this leads to behaviors, and dysregulation, which can make it difficult to learn and focus. Most people would immediately jump into action and provide assistance to any child who has been physically injured. I challenge you to respond with that same expedience in a helpful and healing manner to those children who have unseen injuries.

W.E.B. Dubois so eloquently asked the question in his poignant work *The Souls of Black Folks*: "How does it feel to be a problem?" Imagine being a three-, five-, ten-, or even sixteen-year-old and being labeled a "problem." Some of the children in our schools across the country are told—and truly believe—that they're a problem. Let's work together to ensure that no child ever feels as though he or she is a problem. We want to serve every child as if that child were our own. We want to be fully vested in ensuring children's critical wellness. The average age for participants in the original ACE study was fifty-five years. Your students are far younger than the participants in the original study. If many of the adult participants in the original study were still being impacted by the traumas they endured as children, how then can we expect students to maintain high cognitive function, demonstrate compliance and obedience in school, and be OK at their young age? We can't. And we shouldn't. Social emotional well-being is critical to the healthy development of each and every child. I encourage you to work fervently to ensure that all children in your classroom or school feel that they matter, that they're respected and supported. See them as people first—and then as learners.

KEY TAKEAWAYS

- Demonstrate empathy and compassion with all students.
- Aid in building resilience for young people who may be experiencing severe stressors.
- Identify protective factors and strengths for all students.
- Stop silencing the students who are making the most noise; they are often trying to convey that they need help.[36]
- Choose to reduce and not contribute to the stressors students are already experiencing.

Questions from the Field

In our conversations with teachers, very important questions regarding trauma arise. The following are a few that I hope are helpful in your work with students.

1. *When I know a student has experienced a severe stressor, adversity, or trauma, do I still hold them accountable for their behaviors and/or school work?*

   Absolutely. You do children no favor by not holding them accountable. You can utilize differentiated teaching strategies in your instructional approaches, and restorative justice approaches in your discipline practices. Holding students accountable is another way to demonstrate your love, care, and support for their critical wellness.

2. *What should I do when a student refuses to have his or her needs met?*

   Assess for the safety of the student and others. If the student is safe and there is no threat of harm or danger to the child or others, do not engage in a power struggle with the student. Maintain eyes on the child and give the child some space. After the child has been given some time to reflect and cool off, approach the child calmly, and, in a nonconfrontational manner, discuss the emotions that the child may be feeling and offer appropriate coping strategies to aid in self-regulating.

3. *What can I do right now to help students who are experiencing stressors or trauma?*

   Provide students with a sense of safety and empowerment. Let students know that their voices matter and that you genuinely want to hear them. Demonstrate flexibility and avoid resorting to traditional punitive discipline practices that might entail sending a student to the office or to another colleague's classroom, or taking away recess or lunch. Consider more restorative approaches that still hold students accountable. We don't want students to feel as though they can only be members of our classroom community if they are obedient and compliant.

4. *What can I do when my school administrator and district policies are counter to truly supporting students' healing?*
Focus on the things that you can control. You can control what happens in your classroom. Intervene and advocate on behalf of students when necessary. Ensure that when students are in your classroom, you are affirming their future and creating a culture that supports healing and resilience.

5. *If I suspect that a student has experienced or is experiencing a stressor or trauma, should I ask him or her about it?*
If you suspect that a child is being abused or neglected, it is your duty and responsibility to report your suspicions or knowledge of abuse or neglect of that child to the appropriate child protective services agency in your area. It's not your job to investigate.

Recommended Resources

Craig, S. E. (2016). *Trauma-sensitive schools: Learning communities transforming children's lives, K–5.* New York, NY: Teachers College Press. This book introduces K–5 educators to trauma-sensitive approaches and offers clear explanations of current research as well as practical and creative ideas to help them on their quest to creating trauma-sensitive learning environments.

Craig, S. E., & Sporleder, J. (2017). *Trauma-sensitive schools for the adolescent years: Promoting resiliency and healing, grades 6–12.* New York, NY: Teachers College Press. This book provides secondary educators with practical ideas for how to improve students' achievement by implementing trauma-sensitive approaches to instruction. The authors plainly demonstrate the role that childhood adversity and trauma can play in influencing students' academic success.

Harris, N. B. (2018). *The deepest well: Healing the long-term effects of childhood adversity.* New York, NY: Houghton Mifflin Harcourt. In this book, pediatrician Nadine Burke Harris shares her groundbreaking work of delivering targeted care to vulnerable children, and discusses the connections between toxic stress and lifelong illnesses. This book illuminates just how deeply our bodies can be imprinted by ACEs—abuse, neglect, parental addiction, mental illness, and divorce. Readers will gain insight and tools for helping disrupt the negative health outcomes for young people.

Pritzker, K. (Producer), & Redford, J. (Director). (2015). *Paper tigers* **[Motion picture]. United States: KPJR. Retrieved from www.papertiger-smovie.com.** This documentary follows six students over the course of a school year in a school with a new trauma-sensitive program implemented. The film demonstrates in depth the real-life challenges and traumas that students are experiencing, and the impact those traumas have on their learning, behavior, and overall wellness. The film also does a wonderful job of illustrating empathy in action. School personnel hold students accountable for their behavior and academic achievement while showing empathy, flexibility, and compassion, and offering additional support when required.

Shalaby, C. (2017). *Troublemakers: Lessons in freedom from young children at school.* **New York, NY: New Press.** In this book, author Carla Shalaby, a former elementary schoolteacher, explores the everyday lives of four elementary students who have been deemed "troublemakers." Shalaby challenges the ways we identify and understand so-called problem children. This book demonstrates how educators frequently respond to so-called troublemakers through efforts to moderate, punish, and even medicate them. *Troublemakers* enables us to see school through the lens of children who know firsthand what it means to be labeled a problem.

Smith, D., Fisher, D., & Frey, N. (2015). *Better than carrots or sticks: Restorative practices for positive classroom management.* **Alexandria, VA: ASCD.** This book, written by longtime educators and best-selling authors, offers a comprehensive overview of the origins of restorative practices in schools. These authors do a masterful job of providing a practical guide for creating a cooperative and respectful classroom climate in which students and teachers work through behavioral issues together.

Souers, K., & Hall, P. (2016). *Fostering resilient learners: Strategies for creating a trauma-sensitive classroom.* **Alexandria, VA: ASCD.** Written by a mental health clinician and a veteran educator/principal, this book will help you cultivate a trauma-sensitive learning environment for students across all content areas, grade levels, and educational settings. The authors provide useful information and strategies to aid educators in understanding what trauma is and how it can impact students in the classroom, offer tools to build strong relationships with students, and encourage the adoption of a strengths-based approach when working with students. This book does not overlook the burnout often experienced by educators working with students who have experienced trauma; it offers self-care practices for educators to replenish and flourish.

3

Confronting Implicit Bias and Microaggressions in the Classroom
Distinguishing Intent from Impact

KENJUS T. WATSON

In early August 2017, the "Unite the Right" rally brought together more than one thousand avowed White supremacists in Charlottesville, Virginia, for a collective protest of the city's planned removal of a statue of General Robert E. Lee, leader of the Confederate Army. Clad in gear featuring the slogan "Make America Great Again," the mob marched through the streets chanting such statements as "You [and Jews] will not replace us," "Blood and Soil," "White Lives Matter," "The South Will Rise Again," and "Hail Trump," among other unapologetically racist recitations. Physical violence erupted during the rally, ultimately turning deadly when a twenty-year-old Ohio man accelerated his car into a crowd of counterprotesters, killing thirty-two-year-old Heather Heyer and leaving nineteen others injured, five critically.

Just as students and teachers were preparing to begin the school year, this display of overt White supremacist violence sent shock waves throughout the United States, challenging dominant framings of the US as a progressive democracy with ever-improving racial dynamics. Recently, a concentrated slew of deportations and detainments rocked various communities as hundreds of children with undocumented family members were held in detention centers across the country. These tragic realities present unique challenges for teachers and educators who work with diverse young people and families. In the wake of Charlottesville, an elementary teacher asked Dr. Tyrone Howard whether educators should address this incident, and how. She wondered whether it might be too controversial or potentially harmful to discuss racism with children. "I want to say something to my students about Charlottesville," she said, "but I really don't know what to say, so I probably won't say anything about it unless one of them brings it up."

Dr. Howard offered her a different perspective on how teachers should respond to these moments. He argued that instead of avoiding these teachable moments, educators must

- Equip themselves with sound knowledge on the history of slavery, racism, xenophobia, and the constant quest for equality that many non-White groups in this country faced historically and still struggle for today
- Be willing to stand in the gap between historical racial realities and accepted contemporary narratives of racial dynamics and help students query sources of information. Educators should also realize that there are often no "Kumbaya" moments in discussing issues of race and oppression.
- Be able to help students understand that there is no room for hate in a civil society
- Seek out multiple perspectives, talk to a diversity of people about race-related topics, and acknowledge their own biases

To help all students thrive, educators and other education professionals must take up the call to action and equip themselves to face these tasks through a focused discussion of two interrelated concepts of racism: implicit bias and racial microaggressions. In focusing on student wellness, educators must understand how conscious and unconscious beliefs and attitudes may promote or reduce students' emotional safety. After introducing the concepts of implicit bias and racial microaggressions, I'll outline the current context of racial disparities in schools. I'll follow this with a compelling rationale for honestly and courageously engaging with these precarious realities. One of the key attributes of critical wellness is the ability to feel safe and comfortable in learning situations. To this end, I'll share best practices and challenges involved in anticipating, acknowledging, and interrupting various forms of discrimination and trauma.

Covert Discrimination

The terms **implicit bias** and **microaggressions** are defined differently across academic disciplines.[1] A discussion of the many reasons for these differences is beyond the scope of this chapter. For now, the following definitions are the most accepted by researchers and scholars in the field. Let's start with implicit bias.

Implicit Bias: Unconscious Intent

According to the Kirwan Institute, implicit bias refers to

> the attitudes or stereotypes that affect our understanding, actions, and decisions in an unconscious manner. These biases are typically activated involuntarily, usually without our awareness or intentional control. Additionally, all people are susceptible to displaying some form of implicit bias.[2]

It's helpful to think of implicit bias through the analogy of an iceberg. The tip of the iceberg represents our conscious attitudes, thoughts, and actions. The submerged body of the iceberg, however, accounts for the vast unconscious, the automatic thoughts and beliefs that inform our actions. Our brains use this unconscious space to constantly and rapidly process, categorize, and enable actions based on underlying logic, assumptions, and associations that we've created through years of experience.

Consider the colors green, yellow, and red within the context of driving. The association between these colors and their driving-based messages is so strong that it's difficult to detect any passage of time and the number of steps involved in choosing an appropriate action. These steps include

1. The recognition of different colors on a traffic signal
2. Our recall (memory) of the names/words we typically tie to the colors green, yellow, or red (if our first and only language is English).
3. Our application of further meaning to these words (go, slow, and stop)
4. Our informed action based on this combined knowledge (drive through the intersection or slow the car or come to a complete stop)

Thanks to our learned implicit associations between these colors, terms, meanings, and actions, the entire process of registry, recall, application, and informed action takes place within a few milliseconds. It feels automatic. This is probably for the best. Imagine what would happen if all motorists had to carefully deliberate the meaning of these colors at every intersection! In this way, automatic processing can be helpful for navigating our world. Implicit bias, however, is not only directed toward neutral objects or ideas.

The concept of implicit bias first gained popularity in the late 1970s as researchers tried to understand why individuals who claimed they did not hold prejudiced beliefs or attitudes about marginalized groups (people of color, women, members of the LGBT community, etc.) seemed to discriminate against them anyway.[3] These early studies, as well as recent findings, suggest that whereas explicit intent or bias may be less likely to be admitted or confronted—because it's less socially acceptable and occurs less regularly—unconscious intent or implicit bias is widespread and observable with the help of such tools as the online Implicit Association Test (IAT).[4]

The IAT is a computer-based test that helps individuals better understand their own implicit bias. Test takers are asked to press certain keys that correspond with either a photo of an individual belonging to a distinct social group (e.g., Black people, White people, women, men) or words that have a strong positive or negative meaning (e.g., ugly, beautiful, smart, stupid, dangerous, vomit, safe, lovely). In round one of the IAT, test takers are told to press one key for positive words and/or photos of members of marginalized groups (Black, women, darker people, etc.) and another key for negative words and/or photos of members of dominant groups (White, men, lighter people, etc.). In round two, the test taker is told to switch responses (press one key for negative words and/or members of marginalized groups and another key for positive words or members of dominant groups). Participants' responses in both rounds are timed as researchers examine the difference between how quickly and easily individuals are able to tie positive or negative terms/ideas to marginalized or dominant groups. Figure 3.1 shows a sample screen of the IAT test.

Findings from the IAT, as well as other measures of implicit bias, support the notion that the sometimes-helpful shortcuts utilized by our brains can also result in **stereotyping**. By stereotyping, I mean the process of applying

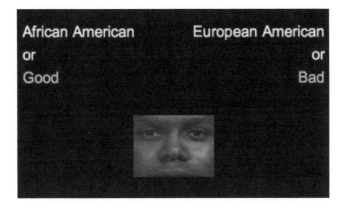

FIGURE 3.1   IAT Test

negative, incomplete, and flawed information to any given member of a socially marginalized group.[5] These unconscious—and often automatic—stereotypes fundamentally affect our judgments and decision-making about different groups. Many researchers believe that these unconscious biases are fueled by negative "symbolic" attitudes, developed over the course of our lives, about socially marginalized groups. These attitudes are informed by messages that we're exposed to every day from a variety of sources—school, media, and conversations with people we trust—that depict people of color, women, LGBTQ individuals, differently abled people, and other marginalized groups in a negative manner.[6]

Therefore, implicit biases are often

- **Hidden.** They reside in our unconscious mind, the part of the brain that many researchers believe is beyond our direct control.
- **Less egalitarian.** Unconscious attitudes are less egalitarian than what we explicitly think about race, class, gender, or sexuality.
- **Self-reinforcing.** Our societal inability to honestly talk about and actively confront issues of race, gender, sexuality, class, and language helps reinforces the implicit bias.[7]

Although most people are loath to consider themselves as unfair or prejudiced, research suggests that none of us are beyond the damaging influence of these discriminatory biases. After two decades of IAT research conducted with millions of participants, we've learned that less than 20 percent of White test takers are able to place positive terms with Black and darker faces. African Americans are only slightly better at 50 percent, a percentage that surprisingly decreases with increasing levels of education. Moreover, additional implicit bias studies have established that, in general, darker people are perceived as larger and more violent than lighter people.[8] Black people are granted a superhuman and dangerous status in relation to how "Black" their name sounds,[9] they continue to be implicitly associated with apes,[10] and they receive less pain medication in emergency situations by virtue of how dark they are.[11]

In sum, although often unconscious, implicit biases reflect unjust worldviews that help maintain and justify oppression.

Racial Microaggressions: Everyday Impact

Renowned Harvard psychiatrist and educator Dr. Chester Pierce first coined the term **racial microaggression** in the late 1960s and early 1970s and developed the subsequent theoretical framework through the mid-1990s. Today, microaggressions are defined as

> everyday manifestations of racism that People of Color encounter in their public and private lives. These subtle assaults can be verbal (or nonverbal), behavioral, and environmental and are often based on not only a Person of Color's race/ethnicity but also how they intersect with other real or perceived differences of gender, class, sexuality, language, immigration status, accent, or surname. The impact of racial microaggressions is cumulative, taking a psychological and physiological toll on those who are targeted.[12]

Microaggressions emerged as a concept after the passage of major civil rights legislation that discouraged overt expressions of racism as acceptable behavior in (most) public spheres. Despite the shift in public policy, Pierce's Black clientele in Cambridge continued to experience hidden forms of everyday racism: "To be black in the United States today means to be socially minimized. For each day blacks are victims of 'offensive mechanisms' which are designed to reduce, dilute, atomize, and encase the hapless into his 'place'" (p. 303).[13]

Today, researchers suggest that these subtle and ambiguous forms of everyday oppression often occur in public settings.[14] In many social or community settings, people of color are perceived as both hypervisible (i.e., they hear car doors lock as they walk by; employees follow them in convenience stores; men catcall them in public; police officers stop them frequently for no apparent reason) and invisible (i.e., they are assumed to be employees and service workers in retail stores and restaurants; pedestrians hold doors for others and not them; they're not called on to offer perspectives in classrooms and official meetings). Thus, unlike other more overt forms of discrimination, microaggressions are subtle "psycho-pollutants" that stress and harm people of color as an everyday manifestation of systemic racism in the United States.

The Basis of Bias and Racial Microaggression

The larger system of racism is supported through racialized structures (historical events), institutions (laws, policies, and agencies), and interpersonal interactions. Implicit bias and racial microaggressions operate at the interpersonal level and function through the everyday interactions between individuals. They stem from a history of oppression that still influences our lives.

Dr. Cheryl Grills discusses this history in a simple yet compelling way in the documentary *Dark Girls*:

> From 1619 to 1865 [Black people] were essentially chattel in this country. . .We were nothing more than animals or beasts. That's 246 years. Imagine that . . . visually: 246 years in the condition of enslavement where . . . we weren't even considered human beings. Then we got emancipation without a plan. From 1865 to 1964 we were really in a position of post-enslavement; people without real rights. And then hits the Civil Rights Movement, 1965 to the present. If we look at that, [we have a large] amount of time in [as enslaved people], [and a small] amount of time out [of slavery]. But of that time out, really only [an even smaller amount] of time out because for most of the time from 1619 to 1965 we had no basic rights in this country. . . We weren't even considered people in the eyes of the law nor in the eyes of our neighbors in the country and in the world.[15]

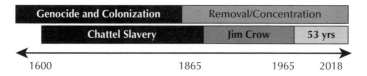

FIGURE 3.2   History of Oppression: A Timeline of US Anti-Blackness and Colonization

This candid and powerful framing of the history of enslavement and oppression is represented on the timeline in Figure 3.2. The figure also includes the context of ongoing genocide and colonial occupation against nations by the US government.

As the figure shows, officially sanctioned chattel slavery in the United States lasted for nearly three hundred years and was followed by another hundred years of overt anti-Black racial apartheid. There has been a total of only fifty-four years in which Black people (and by extension other people of color) are considered "human citizens" by a government that continues to occupy ill-gotten land at the expense of millions of Indigenous lives. Considering this timeline, we can think of implicit bias and microaggressions as the toxic residue of these events. We can also consider them to be everyday reminders and reinforcers of people of color's history of suffering and structural positions in an inherently unjust society. That all of us may be susceptible at any given time to parrot, echo, or enact the violence that undergirds the geographic, political, and social organization of the United States is predictable. In some ways, unfortunately, it's even logical, given the imbalance of time spent within and outside the states of legal slavery and racial apartheid.

Intent versus Impact: A Distinction

The terms *implicit bias* and *microaggressions* are often used interchangeably to refer to hidden racism. In reality, however, they actually describe two different yet related dynamics in subtle discrimination. In hopes of further differentiating implicit bias from microaggressions and prompting reflection on how they might show up in our classrooms, consider an analogy based on *What Would You Do?*, an ABC network television program. This is a hidden-camera show featuring actors in public settings performing scenarios of conflict or illegal activity in

FIGURE 3.3   What Would You Do?

close proximity to bystanders who believe that the interactions they're observing are real. The focus of the show is to observe whether and how the unknowing bystanders will react to the performance of the actors, as well as to hear about the motivations for their reactions (or lack thereof). Variations are also included, such as changing the genders, the races, or the clothing of the actors performing the scene, to see whether bystanders react differently. The host of the show appears at the end of each scenario to interview bystanders and witnesses about their reactions. Let's participate in a What Would You Do? scenario using the scene in Figure 3.3.

Consider implicit bias in the first version of our scenario. Our actor is the person walking in the top left-hand corner, and the unknowing bystander is in the bottom left-hand corner of the picture. As the actor walks down the sidewalk, the bystander suddenly crosses the street. At this moment, the hidden cameras become visible and the host of our *What Would You Do?* appears, asking the bystander, "Why do you think you *decided* to cross the street just now?" Consider the likely responses of this understandably surprised individual. They might say

- I wanted to go to a store on this side of the street.
- I thought that vehicle was my car.
- My movement wasn't deliberate. I just felt like crossing the street.

We know the individual might respond in one of these three ways because research suggests most people are unlikely to notice their discriminatory actions.[16] In other words, rarely will someone self-report a decision they make as informed by bias stemming from exposure to damaging portrayals of historically marginalized groups. This clear mismatch between behavior and self-awareness fuels the study of implicit bias. In this way, implicit bias focuses on the unconscious *intentions* of *perpetrators* of automatic and subtle discriminatory actions.

Now let's consider another scenario to better understand microaggressions. We'll switch the role of bystander and actor in our What Would You Do? scenario. In this second version, the person at the bottom left of the picture will now become our actor who is helping conduct the social experiment, and the person at the top left of the scene is the unknowing bystander. The camera crew and host appear after the actor crosses the street. However, this time, they turn their attention to the unknowing bystander and ask, "How are you feeling after the individual crossed the street away from you?" Again, considering the context and timing of the question, this person may reply

- I feel frustrated and/or hurt.
- I don't feel much of anything. I'm used to this happening, especially in this area of town.
- I didn't even notice that the other person crossed the street.

This scenario and question, and the possible answers, are tied to the concept of racial microaggressions. Recall that implicit bias concerns the seemingly automatic, unconscious intent of perpetrators of subtle racism. When we examine microaggressions, we focus on the harmful *impact* the microaggressive assault has on the *target* of everyday racism (see Figure 3.4).

According to researchers, "Racial microaggressions can be best explained as the enactment of implicit biases on People of Color."[17]

In the Classroom

Once we are armed with this understanding of unconscious racism, our challenge as educators is to recognize how these moments play out

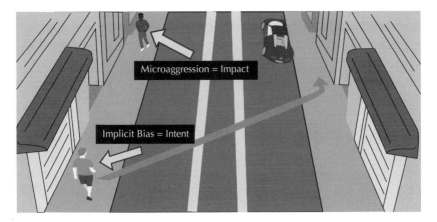

FIGURE 3.4   What Would You Do? Take Two

in our work with young people. To help you do so, I encourage you to reflect on instances when you may have knowingly or unknowingly "crossed the street" on or away from the students of color with whom you work.

The Unconscious Intent of Bias

Unfortunately, when researchers study implicit bias in K–12 settings, they discover unequal treatment and low expectations directed at students of color. Black preschool students are repeatedly suspended at disproportionate rates compared to their White peers.[18] Relatedly, by the time they're five years old, Black girls are already perceived by educators to be older and less innocent than White girls of the same age.[19] Black boys and girls are five times more likely to be suspended than their White peers for equally or less serious conduct.[20] Students of color are disproportionately tracked into lower-skilled courses and rarely placed in advanced or gifted-and-talented tracks. Teachers also routinely mispronounce and alter the names of children of color to more Europeanized versions.[21] Students of color are also taught from European-centered curricula and implicitly encouraged to mimic White, middle-class values and mannerisms in language, dress, and ideology.[22] Moreover, all educators are capable of these biases, regardless of their overt intentions or racial identities, as we have all internalized aspects of our own racist schooling experiences.

The Harmful Impact of Microaggressions

These accumulated microaggressions sink students' self-esteem, stunt their academic progress, and disrupt their immediate and long-term health.[23] Mispronouncing or haphazardly changing Black and brown students' names may seem relatively harmless. However, this persistent mistake is actually grounded in a long history of racial and cultural oppression that can have a lasting impact on the self-perception and worldview of a child. In addition, the higher rates of suspensions and expulsions of Black and Latinx youth has been tied to their disproportionately high rates of incarceration.[24] These and related forms of race-related stress are social toxins that increase susceptibility to disease among people of color and generate racial disparities in health. For example, Black and Latinx individuals who reported experiencing everyday discrimination in school when they were twelve years old had higher levels of cortisol in their systems in their thirties compared to peers who experienced less discrimination.[25] Disrupted cortisol levels are associated with higher risk for life-threatening health problems, such as cardiovascular disease and diabetes. A study under way by one of the authors on the impact of racial microaggressions on Black college students suggests that everyday racism is a damaging stressor that may be related to cellular degeneration and rapid aging.[26] These results echo similar studies on the biological impact of racism.

The unfortunate reality is that, despite the best intentions of educators, children of color are frequently treated less favorably and subsequently endure serious consequences within and beyond K–12 spaces.

Critical Wellness Best Practices

As educators in the current political climate, we find ourselves at what seems like an unprecedented juncture concerning racism, nationalism, gender, sexuality, and other oppression-related issues that often show up in our classrooms. History teaches us, however, that these realities (and the courageous efforts to dismantle them) have constituted the very thread of the fabric of the United States since its inception.[27]Moreover, wide-scale integration did not occur following the landmark *Brown v. Board of Education* Supreme Court decision,[28] and students of color have been the majority of the school-going population since 2014.[29] Given these facts, the seemingly weekly identity-related *crises* that have emerged since November 2016 may be better understood as *opportunities* for K–12 teachers, practitioners, and leaders to mindfully join the struggle to establish more just, loving, and dignified futures for historically marginalized students and communities. Teachers can take tangible steps toward this aim by attending to the aforementioned history, expanding their capacities to facilitate conversations about race, and acknowledging their own biases. These suggestions are interrelated and align with the following best practices for decreasing implicit bias and interrupting the impact of microaggressions in classroom spaces:

1. Acceptance
2. Belief
3. Anticipatory action

Let's take a closer look at each of these three best practices, including practical steps to help incorporate them in a classroom setting.

Acceptance

The first step to limiting unconscious bias and microaggressions is to acknowledge our likely complicity in interpersonal racism, given our socialization within an environment that is historically, structurally, and institutionally racist. In her best-selling book *Why Are All the Black Kids Sitting Together in the Cafeteria?*, Beverly Tatum offers a helpful anecdote when she likens the influence and integration of racism in our society to the amount of smog in a polluted area.[30] The air in Los Angeles is smoggy. That's a fact. Living in the city, my status as a "smog-breather" is a foregone conclusion. This is true whether I take public transport, ride a bicycle, drive an emissions-free vehicle, or operate a diesel truck. Similarly, the structure of the United States is decidedly anti-Black, anti-Indigenous, and White supremacist, given the history of chattel slavery, genocidal colonization, and racial apartheid that undergirds the creation and progress of the nation. Overtly stated racist policies were rendered illegal only fifty-four years ago. Thus the propensity of those of us socialized or living within this space to be racist is a foregone conclusion. This historical reality and its residue continue to operate as the root of our contemporary problems. It's therefore important to learn more about this history in order to truly accept our ability to reproduce its influence. Such acceptance allows educators to make more mindful decisions about how they might use different practices to resist participating in oppression.

Acceptance comes from knowledge. In this vein, I encourage teachers to take the Implicit Association Test (IAT). As previously mentioned, the IAT provides insight into one's potential implicit bias across a number of domains, including race, class, gender, sexuality, and religion. It takes approximately ten minutes to complete any given test, and you can take them as many times as you like. Test takers are also anonymous. Beyond gaining this individual-level knowledge, learning more about the history of racism in the United States and accepting that White, middle-class, male, heterosexual narratives and perspectives undergird what dominant culture considers to be normal, neutral, good, and right enables teachers to make decidedly different decisions that disrupt this status quo.

In order to disrupt this regime of knowledge, educators are encouraged to imagine their pedagogical materials, classroom setup, and behavior management strategies as powerful mirrors for their students. Some important questions to consider: Do these mirrors reflect the marginalized students with whom you work? Can the students see themselves and their families, their histories of resistance, resilience, and healing from the centuries of oppression represented in the spaces in which they are being educated? Try conducting an audit of the physical space and pedagogical materials with these questions in mind. An important place to begin is to provide space and time to learn the correct pronunciation of students' names. In addition, we know that Black and brown youth are often seen as disruptive, disrespectful, older, and in need of less nurturing.

Belief

The second recommendation for disrupting bias and microaggressions is to believe those who may be harmed. A few years ago, a colleague shared an experience he had that reminded him of the interplay between implicit bias and microaggressions. He was helping his five-year-old son, Jeremy, with an art project. They were using construction paper, scissors, and glue. While using the scissors, Jeremy glanced away for a moment and ended up cutting his dad's finger. Surprised by the slit on his hand, his dad said, "Ouch! Jeremy, you just cut my finger."

Jeremy's head jerked back toward the paper, his dad's finger, and the supposed weapon in his own small hand. My colleague recounted how he could see Jeremy's mind at work as the young boy assessed the scene. Jeremy replied, "But I didn't mean to!"

My colleague also relayed that Jeremy's response is both predictable and understandable. It is predictable because he knew and believed that his son did not intend to cut his finger. It was understandable because my colleague could do the mental math and translate his statement to its likely intended meaning: "I don't want to be the cause of your pain, however small it may be." Jeremy's response is also puzzling and inappropriate, however, given the actual outcomes of his actions. In other words, Jeremy's professed lack of intention was unrelated to and thus ineffective in addressing the cut on his dad's finger or the blood on the table. This mismatch was also understandable given that Jeremy was five years old at the time. With this in mind, my colleague simply let Jeremy know in that moment, "A better thing to say when we hurt another person by accident is 'sorry.' Now, let's clean up the blood!"

Although the moral of this story seems relatively straightforward, we typically have a hard time applying its lesson to incidents of implicit bias and microaggression. The vast majority of us have a natural urge to limit our capacity to harm others through our overt intentions. Believing that we cannot hurt others if we do not mean to, though, centers our intention (bias) as the most important component in any interpersonal interaction. And, as in the example of the art project, such denial of intention does not address the potential impact (microaggression) on the person who has been harmed. We're all susceptible to enacting bias. Therefore, if we learn to *accept* that our unconscious foundation has been informed by racist socialization and structures, we should also *believe* young people when they tell us they're experiencing harm from a microaggression.

Teachers can model belief by developing community agreements or ground rules with their students. Such ground rules typically enable students and teachers to cocreate an environment in which all community members promise to work on developing accountability when they harm others while working toward a more respectful, shared, and collective space of engagement. In an effort to model accountability and the procedures for limiting harm, it may be helpful for teachers to talk with their students openly about times when they have incidentally engaged in bias and when they've been harmed by such bias. Saying "I believe you" and "I'm sorry" when we're informed of our unconscious bias and invoking the community agreements in a process of restoration can go a long way toward engendering trust with students and cultivating an environment that better prepares them to contribute to a more equitable, just, and loving future.

Anticipatory Action

The third recommendation for decreasing bias and interrupting microaggressions in educational spaces is to take anticipatory action against them. Experiencing a microaggression is akin to having a person identify and aggravate a sore scar on your body and, in the same breath, deny that you feel any pain. Part of the reason why microaggressions are harmful is that they remind people of color of their history of suffering and simultaneously (and somewhat paradoxically) conceal and deny that there has been a significant history of oppression. This is evident when we consider the timeline in Figure 3.2. The timeline is simple, straightforward, and true. However, it may have resonated as surprising and radical to some because many of us have been socialized to think of US history through a lens that downplays and mystifies the harm done to people of color.

Modern-day implicit bias and microaggressions echo that history. For example, the history of enslavement and apartheid is involved in the fact that Black students are disciplined more regularly and severely than other students for less serious offenses. The same history is involved in the fact that darker-skin students are more often referred to special education services compared to lighter-skin students. The history of colonization, boarding schools, and annexation are involved in the practice of changing Latinx students' names or reprimanding them for talking to each other in languages other than English. These same histories, layered with western notions of gender and sexuality, are involved in the fact that Black and Latina girls are sent home disproportionately often relative to White girls for dress code violations. The same history of forcing a binary system of gender and sexuality is inherent in school procedures and practices that ignore and deride gender-nonconforming expressions and identities.

Again, it may be surprising—or even radical—to understand these data-based realities as historically grounded, harmful microaggressions. The goal, though, is to move beyond surprise at the occurrence of everyday racism into a space where we accept that discrimination is happening regardless of our best intentions or perceived level of consciousness (which has had only about fifty-four years of institutional support). Once we're able to grasp these moments as tied to past and ongoing practices of exclusion, we can interrupt and limit our capacity to obtusely aggravate a generational wound and simultaneously deny the subsequent pain.

This aligns with Chester Pierce's advice that individuals should be taught to recognize microaggressions and construct their future by taking appropriate action at each instance of recognition.[31] Armed with *acceptance* and *belief*, educators can begin to take *anticipatory action* that challenges bias and lessens the harm of microaggressions. Some teachers may be familiar with "equity sticks." This practice involves writing each student's name on a craft stick and placing the sticks in plain sight at the beginning of each day. They will set aside a stick when they call on the matched student. This simple practice enables teachers to more reliably track how equitably they engage their students. It was developed as an anticipatory response to the implicit bias of less engagement with young boys of color. According to Pierce's advice, educators should recognize the enactment of an unintended implicit bias, acknowledge the harm of the microaggression on the outcomes for students, and take appropriate, anticipatory action to preempt the bias and lessen the harm.

Teachers and other educational practitioners might consider taking the IAT to establish which biases are more present. Then they should reflect on strategies to interrupt the bias and implement these strategies within their learning spaces. This process of recognition, reflection, and action is suggested by other experts who study microaggressions. Relatedly, it's important to equip students of color with similar recognition, reflection, and action tools.

As a response to microaggressions, racial microaffirmations are emerging as another form of anticipatory action. Racial microaffirmations are the often subtle verbal or nonverbal strategies people of color consciously use that acknowledge and affirm one another's value, integrity, and shared humanity.[32] According to Pérez Huber, these affirmations are:

> (1) Verbal and/or non-verbal affirmations exchanged between People of Color, (2) layered affirmations based on race and its intersections with other subordinated social identities, and (3) cumulative affirmations that have positive psychological and physiological effects when experienced by People of Color over a lifetime. These affirmations are manifested in the subtle nods, smiles, embraces, and use of language shared within Communities of Color, in both public and private spheres, that can express acknowledgement, affirm self-worth, and engender support.[33]

These everyday affirmations are a response to racial microaggressions. As such, they acknowledge the resilience and life of those who are most marginalized by oppression. Therefore, it's crucial to cultivate educational spaces where these types of affirmations can proliferate, whether between students or between key staff and students.

KEY TAKEAWAYS

- Totalizing anti-Blackness and unmitigated colonization are historically cemented into the very structure of the US, including its formative and socializing institutions (e.g., schools). Implicit bias and microaggressions are employed daily and serve as what Chester Pierce referred to as mundane "terrors, tortures, and disasters" that echo, reify, and reflect (and concurrently deny) the structure of historical suffering inflicted on people of color
- Implicit bias and microaggressions are, however, distinct concepts of everyday, interpersonal oppression, distinguished by the focus of analysis. Implicit bias is about the *intent* (conscious or unconscious) of the perpetrators of mundane discrimination, whereas microaggressions attune our attention to the *impact* that everyday forms of oppression have on marginalized people. In understanding this difference, it is important to ensure that we continuously uplift, trust, and address

the very real *impact* of discrimination on people of color whether or not we can clearly discern or prove the explicit *intent* of others (or ourselves) to inflict harm.

- Educators should rigorously educate themselves on the history and contemporary nature of oppression in the US and the harmful impact of these systems on the lives of the young people with whom they work. Teachers should also accept the likelihood that, in occupying a still toxic environment, they have or eventually will have internalized and expressed noxious, biased beliefs about various communities of color.
- In order to undermine the impact of our internalization of bias, we should accept our possible complicity in these events, believe young people when they say they've been harmed by an enactment of microaggression, set up racially literate and communicative classroom environments that allow for appropriate naming of racism and accountable redress, and anticipate/buffer against microaggressions through everyday microaffirmations of the students we work with.

Questions from the Field

In our conversations with teachers, very important questions regarding implicit bias and microaggressions arise. The following are a few that I hope are helpful in your work with students.

1. *How can someone have "unconscious intent"?*
   Implicit bias is a somewhat counterintuitive concept because it requires a suspension of a core message taught to many individuals from a young age: *people are inherently in control of (and thus responsible for) their own thoughts and actions.* In response, I invite you to pause for a moment, close your eyes, place your hand on your chest, and listen to and feel the sound of your heart beating.
   I'll give you few moments . . .

What you hear and feel is one of the most powerful and essential organs in the human body working to pump oxygen-carrying and life-giving blood throughout your veins.

Speaking of oxygen, I now invite you to bring your overt attention to your breath. Try to inhale air for a count of three seconds, hold your breath for another count of three seconds, and finally release the air for one more count of three seconds. You can do this a few times if you like and see whether you can notice an increase in your awareness of the breath you are taking in and releasing.

The interrelated physiological processes of palpating and breathing we just engaged are critical for humans to remain alive. They function, however, seemingly at the individual will of our brains, wholly unconnected to the overt attention or control of our active consciousness. Thank goodness for this! Could you imagine preparing students to participate in an experiential classroom activity and at the same time being completely responsible for actively and consciously telling your heart to beat, while also remembering to breathe? Thankfully, most individuals' brains do this heavy lifting whether they're conscious of it or not.

The same can be said of many other brain-regulated processes, including our "social actions," such as categorization. We may be more or less conscious of placing other human beings (including youth) into race, gender, and other identity-related boxes. Our general lack of awareness of these actions, however, does not limit their continued occurrence. Further, these boxes are embedded within and informed by a history of oppression and by contemporary inequality. Thus the term *unconscious intent* is an attempt to name our potential complicity in echoing oppressive frameworks in our actions even when we don't necessarily want to. It's an imperfect term, but it describes an evidenced phenomenon.

2. *Doesn't micro mean "small"? Some of these examples seem really overt and are more like macroaggressions. Why are you calling these different moments "aggressions" when they could be unconscious? Doesn't an aggressive act need to be intentional?*

This set of questions concerns the naming of microaggressions and are posed rather frequently during and after professional development workshops. In order to better understand the nomenclature (naming) of microaggressions, it is important to note that Chester Pierce started working on the framework in the 1960s.

Pierce first used the term "offensive mechanisms" to describe these events. The Harvard psychiatrist had actually played football for the school when he was a student. In fact, Pierce broke the color line at Harvard in the 1940s when he became the first Black person on a White team to play in a football game against another team south of the Mason-Dixon line. Theorizing with a lens informed by his collegiate athletic career as an offensive tackle, Pierce compared Black people's existence in public space to defensive linemen who endure frequent hits and punishment from offensive mechanisms designed to wear them down. Football was the analogy that gave us microaggressions!

These are called "aggressions" because they name the harmful *impact* on the targets. Pierce's framing and the subsequent work that it influenced are less concerned with the intention of the perpetrator. Also, according to Pierce, these "hits" are really, "micro in name only because their very number requires an effort that is incalculable." In other words, the *micro* in *microaggressions* doesn't mean small or less than. Instead, it means everyday, incessant, and insidious. See Figure 3.5 for an arrangement of microaggressions compared to meso- and macroaggressions.

The concentric circles show different levels of racial oppression. **Macroaggressions (or mechanisms of structural racism)** are placed at the outermost and foundational layer because the US came into being through the theft and genocide of Indigenous people, as well as hundreds of years of slavery and unadulterated violence against captured Africans and their descendants. The ongoing macroaggressions against Indigenous people and Blacks (along with other marginalized groups) are sanctioned, justified,

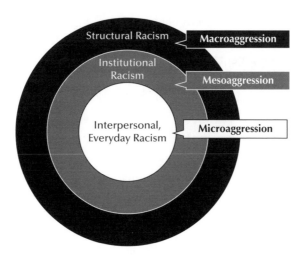

FIGURE 3.5   Levels of Racial Oppression

and rendered invisible by racially discriminatory policies and institutions at the **mesoaggression (middle or institutional racism) level**. **Racial microaggressions (everyday racism)** are the frequent interpersonal interactions, experiences, and messages that echo and reinforce the macro- and mesoaggressions by reminding people of color of their historical positions within an inherently unjust society.

3. *What can we do to stop implicit bias and microaggressions?*

   At the start of professional development or professional learning opportunities, I tell teachers that we will be discussing aspects related to the harm of everyday racism. I then jokingly relay to them that I can't promise we'll bring an end to racism in the ensuing two hours, but that I'll do my best. I say this because, in truth, despite my best efforts to provide evidenced and tangible support around these issues, there's simply no quick fix or effective lesson plan to bring an end to the disease of which microaggressions are simply one symptom. We've all been socialized for many years into a system that is engrained into the very breath of the nation.

I think it's better to embrace this as an opportunity to engage in an "unlearning" that will be lifelong.

Simultaneously, although subtle racism processes typically operate automatically, the mindfulness exercises we did in question 1 demonstrate that we're able to interject our overt attention to automatic functioning when we're made of aware of its quiet work. This is an important reminder that when we pay mindful attention to the likelihood of bias, we may be able to be more influential in disrupting it. I want to also reiterate the importance of the recognition, reflection, and response process in helping us pay closer attention to everyday racism. Further, the suggestions related to acceptance, belief, and anticipatory action are paramount to mitigating harm. Finally, I cannot overstate the importance of microaffirmations—those subtle words or actions that express acknowledgment and affirm self-worth for those who've been marginalized by society. Together, these actions can go a long way toward ensuring critical wellness and creating a space where all students can thrive.

Recommended Resources

Implicit Association Test. Educators can access multiple versions of the Implicit Association Test at www.implicit.harvard.edu and take these tests as often as they like to get a better understanding of their potential bias. There are also guides linked to the IAT that may be helpful should educators decide to use the task in a lesson plan with their students.

Kirwan Institute for the Study of Race and Ethnicity (www.kirwaninstitute.osu.edu). This research hub at Ohio State University is an excellent resource for information about implicit bias. It includes yearly reports, up-to-date findings on the concept, and a special focus on K–12 classrooms.

Kang, J. (2013). Immaculate perception. TED. Retrieved from www.youtube.com/watch?v=9VGbwNI6Ssk. There are several TED Talks regarding implicit bias readily available through a search on YouTube. I recommend this talk by legal scholar Jerry Kang. It is a straightforward, engaging, and helpful guide for thinking through the concept.

Pérez Huber, L., & Solórzano, D. G. (2015). *Microaggressions: What they are, what they are not, and why they matter* (Latino Policy & Issues Brief, No. 30). UCLA Chicano Studies Research Center. This policy brief provides an important grounding for the framework of microaggressions.

Watson, K. T., & Pérez Huber, L. (2016). *Micro in name only: Looking back to move forward in microaggressions research* (Research Brief, No. 3). Center for Critical Race Studies at UCLA. I coauthored this short piece with Lindsay Pérez Huber as a follow-up to her and Solórzano's earlier brief. It is helpful in further detailing the history of microaggressions as well as the recognition, reflection, and response model.

Kohli, R., & Solórzano, D. G. (2012). Teachers, please learn our names! Racial microaggressions and the K–12 classroom. *Race, Ethnicity and Education, 15,* 441–462. doi:10.1080/13613324.2012.674026. This article provides insight into the reality and impact of microaggressions in K–12 educational spaces. It is a good deep dive for folks interested in learning more about how these offensive mechanisms operate in school settings, and it offers helpful recommendations.

4

Designing Culturally Responsive Learning Experiences

TONIKIAA ORANGE

A tension arises in schools when educators are asked to create spaces that support, acknowledge, and bring to life the cultures of their diverse student population. It shows itself in educators' responses to this request. They respond by repurposing "best teaching practices," by reiterating dominant mainstream norms and beliefs about what teaching and learning should look and feel like for students, or by engaging in the types of student- and parent-blaming sentiments from which a deficit ideology of race and culture often emerges. Meanwhile, many of their students associate school with inauthentic experiences and control over mind and body. Because of this, school becomes an experience distant from the way they navigate and negotiate the world.

The tension caused by this lack of culturally diverse educational spaces stems from a variety of factors. For one, US public schools were designed to serve monolingual and monocultural agendas (i.e., English-speaking, middle-class, White students). This leaves students of color and other marginalized students to assimilate in order to succeed, often at the expense of their own culture and language.[1] Also, the tension arises from the lack of attention schools pay to supporting their teachers' understanding of how race and culture impact their instruction and students' learning. Students are continuously asked to shift their cultural identity to fit the mainstream classroom environment, while schools slowly shift policies and teaching practices to support the changing demographics and societal inequities that show up in classrooms.[2]

It's not lost on educators that many marginalized students of color are overrepresented in intervention and remedial classes, credit recovery courses, and special education.[3] Students are often placed in these spaces due to cultural misunderstandings and the classification of their cultural behaviors as "defiant" or noncompliant as compared to traditional White middle-class ways of being in school. In turn, students are deprived of participating in classes such as art or music, and even recess if they're not compliant in classrooms. This is done even though schools have failed to support and create a learning environment where students' cultural attributes are considered assets instead of deficits. For marginalized students of color, the social aspect of school is part of the learning experience, and they're hurt when we take away courses and activities that inherently lend themselves to social engagement. Instead, these courses are substituted for more time in classrooms that are focused on core content and that often feel disengaging and disconnected from students' lives. I haven't encountered many students who get enthusiastic about going to "intervention," but I've met plenty who can't wait for recess or lunch. The enthusiasm that students feel at recess can be captured in our classrooms if educators critically reflect on how they teach and are intentional in connecting what they teach to the lived experiences of their students.

To help students thrive in schools, we need teachers who can create culturally responsive learning experiences. In order to create engaging and loving environments for the most marginalized students, we need teachers to pose problems and ask questions that enable them to critique current structures and practices in classrooms. But our educational system sets teachers up as problem solvers instead of problem posers. To create culturally responsive learning experiences, teachers need to ask questions that challenge structures, rethink systems, and confront their own and others' mindsets about learning. The process of creating culturally responsive learning experiences is inherently about student wellness. It forces us first to understand that our students are not problems to be solved but rather young people who need to be understood, loved, and provided with a reimagined educational space that supports their diverse cultural needs.

Culture as the Catalyst

If supporting students to thrive emotionally, academically, and socially is a central goal of the teaching process, then teachers must consciously think about how culture shapes the ways students see and interact with the world around them. And, as one novice third-grade teacher from Los Angeles told my colleagues and me during our research, culture is not race—and it goes beyond ethnicity. "Culture deals with additional aspects, such as time, child rearing, social interactions between peers, cooperation and collaboration, and so on," she explained. "A shift I've seen in myself is being more aware of how students respond or react to certain situations. When I go into the classroom, I look at opportunities for various ways students can engage and respond besides raising hands, such as incorporating movement, call and response, or supporting more collaboration. I realize these are all connected to culture."

Education scholar Geneva Gay refers to culture as "a dynamic system of social values, cognitive codes, behavioral standards, worldviews and beliefs used to give order and meaning to our lives as well as the lives of others."[4] Supporting teachers in examining the connection between culture and learning, and then developing a knowledge base around the complexities of culture, can catalyze greater equity, student wellness, social emotional learning, and the disruption of existing dominant norms that act as barriers to success for culturally diverse students.

Culturally responsive teachers use the students' culture to create authentic learning experiences that transform educational spaces into learning environments that *intentionally* acknowledge and sustain the cultural dexterity of diverse students. They position those same students for academic, ethical, political, and social growth because they intentionally deconstruct old paradigms and create new ones that make students' cultural assets central to teaching and learning. These teachers better understand the various cultural factors and experiences that influence the ways students learn best, so they think critically and act intentionally to address issues of inequity in their schools.

When deciding how best to serve all students, educators must be willing to examine what is often overlooked. They must focus on what is invisible in school spaces (cultural values, beliefs, norms, race, bias, etc.) when deciding how and what to teach and what policies to enact. They can't talk about academic achievement, discipline, content, and the like without understanding how the invisible directly impacts the visible. Figure 4.1 illustrates how we tend to focus on what's above the line because it's easily seen and allows us to collect quantifiable data. But in reality, what's under the line is the anchor for all the work that takes place in schools. Teachers who want to create

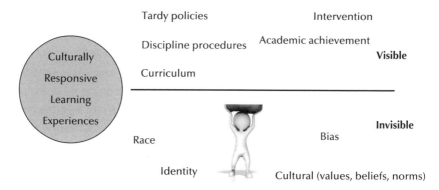

FIGURE 4.1   Making the Invisible Visible

culturally responsive learning experiences for students start below the line by first making the invisible visible.

This journey starts with educators first investigating and examining their own identity, bias, and cultural values and beliefs—and, thus, beginning to view themselves and their students as dynamic, complex, and constantly changing. Then educators can begin to dismantle their **deficit thinking**, or those unquestioned assumptions and stereotypes that lead educators to assume that students of differing backgrounds have a deficit that they need to fix. After invalidating deficit thinking, educators can begin to provide more authentic and purposeful experiences. Students naturally view themselves through the lens of their own culture, rather than as an object of schooling, so this work to heighten teachers' ability to be culturally responsive will lead to more students who are self-confident and who enact critical consciousness, self-care, and love. Through culturally responsive teaching, teachers can shift the way teaching and learning look and feel for all their students.

What Is Culturally Responsive Teaching?

Culturally responsive teaching is "a pedagogy that empowers students intellectually, socially, emotionally, and politically by using cultural and historical referents to convey knowledge, to impart skills, and to change attitudes."[5] Although culture is taught implicitly through linguistic forms and traditions, this approach intentionally and explicitly incorporates "the culture of the learner into the academic and social context of schools in ways that facilitate and support academic learning and cultural identity and promote personal, human, and social development."[6] It acknowledges the complexities and fluidity of culture, and it focuses on changing the mindsets of teachers to understand the connection between culture and learning.[7] It pushes teachers to build greater knowledge about their own cultural identity and its influence on how they teach and how they see learning happen in classrooms.

This requires a deliberate effort, one that's not always easy in the moment. "My mindset is a bit more mindful of others and stopping to think about the situation instead of just acting right away," one veteran high school counselor who works in Los Angeles told us. "I'm trying to be more aware of why I react certain ways and understand more about students and their culture. And I'm also trying to relate to their experiences and make connections. I look at what success really is for each student, not the whole group." Only when teachers, like this counselor, acknowledge their own cultural lenses and work to understand how their cultural identities impact their teaching can they move to provide culturally responsive learning experiences that are deliberate, purposeful, and responsive to all students.

Culturally responsive teaching requires educators to do the following:

- Examine their cultural identities and know how those identities influence their ideals about teaching and learning
- Acknowledge their bias and its influence on their beliefs about students
- Know that teaching is not neutral or color-blind and understand that the intersectionality of race, ethnicity, socioeconomics, gender, religion, and so on impacts how they think about teaching and the learner. Color blindness disregards the importance of how these identities shape the educational experience of diverse students.
- Understand that ways of knowing are varied, and they're defined through one's own cultural context. Notions of participation, engagement, communication patterns, respect, and use of language are culturally based.
- Know that culture adds strength and perspective to a learning community. Exposing divergent points of view and opening various ways to see content and concepts strengthen students' ability to critique their own views and create new ways to see the world.

- Create culturally relevant, authentic content and use teaching strategies that support the communication patterns, language, and learning styles of their diverse students.
- Intentionally engage students in complex and controversial matters that help them analyze and critique sociopolitical contexts.
- Create and build a school environment that practices "culturally responsive care."[8] **Culturally responsive care** is caring *for*, not just caring *about*, "the personal well-being and academic success of ethnically diverse students. *Caring about* conveys feelings of concern for one's state of being, *caring for* is active engagement in doing something to positively affect it. Thus, it encompasses a combination of concern, compassion, commitment, responsibility and action."[9]

It's critical to note that culturally responsive teaching is action oriented, and it intentionally disrupts existing practices and policies that perpetuate inequity. It honors students and helps bridge them to improved academic achievement, social consciousness, and critical reflection of their own and others' cultural norms and beliefs. It redefines and can transform the school experience for diverse students by leveraging their ways of being and knowing to increase opportunities for success and overall student wellness.

Maintaining Culturally Responsive Teaching in Classrooms

Culturally responsive teaching requires continuous examination of teachers' implicit and explicit biases, a topic touched on in chapter 3. To counter bias, refute deficit perspectives, and combat racial stereotypes, culturally responsive teachers need to engage in an inquiry process that pushes them to continuously examine their identity and question bias or deficit thinking in themselves, in their colleagues, and throughout the classroom environment. "I was reading the kids a book, and in the story, all of the books in the world had been wiped clean of words," one Los Angeles elementary school teacher told us. She went on to explain:

> This made the whole world "dumb." As I was reading, I noticed a lot of things about what the author believes "dumb language" to be. Several of the patterns that are common to Chicano English and African American English came up. For example, one character was called

"dumb" because he said, "I don't read no more." A few years ago, I wouldn't have thought much of this, but now I recognize it as a perpetuation of White supremacy in the form of language shaming. Just by reading this book as first graders, these kids are starting to internalize what is "intelligent" and what is "dumb" language. So then what happens when they walk into a community that uses these language patterns that they now have a deficit view on? They make assumptions about intelligence. It's very frustrating.

The inquiry process through which educators examine their own identity and then critically examine their classrooms and curricula takes place in **reciprocal learning partnerships (RLPs)**. To get a better sense of how RLPs work, see Figure 4.2.

The RLP framework supports and empowers educators to work together to explicitly identify inequitable teaching practices in classrooms and then collaboratively develop actions that will foster the types of culturally responsive experiences that improve academic outcomes for culturally diverse students.

By centering the classroom as the place to leverage change for culturally responsive teachers, RLPs build teachers' capacity to critically reflect in

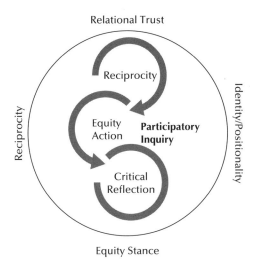

FIGURE 4.2   Reciprocal Learning Partnerships Framework

partnerships, hold equity-focused conversations, and coconstruct actions that help eliminate oppressive and dominant ways of thinking about teaching and learning. The framework prepares teachers to proactively shift their teaching practices, policies, and/or classroom structures in order to increase culturally diverse students' opportunities for success. It requires that they see the institution of schooling as fundamentally political rather than merely physical and then focus on the dismantling and disruption of the cycle of inequity through culturally responsive teaching.

Participatory inquiry, which lies at the center of the RLP framework, is the method by which culturally responsive teachers—in partnership with colleagues and/or administrators—learn how to continually critique and question their beliefs. Participatory inquiry acknowledges each person's agency and engages each person in the exchange of ideas, the creation of new knowledge, the examination of perspectives and assumptions, and the *action* needed to support culturally responsive teaching and equitable outcomes for students. The participatory inquiry cycle consists of the following:

- **Reciprocal dialogue:** a two-way exchange of ideas and knowledge in which each person challenges and explores his or her worldview with shared norms and open, authentic communication.
- **Equity action:** the process by which inquiry moves to action and contributes to improved outcomes for culturally diverse students. Action is directly linked to empowering and changing the lived experiences of diverse students and those most marginalized in classrooms and schools.
- **Critical reflection:** an examination and awareness of our perspectives and biases, along with the subsequent challenging of our assumptions through repeated cycling between action, dialogue, and reflection.

For educators to engage in participatory inquiry, they must first have complex and often difficult conversations about race, identity, their role in students' lives, and other factors that influence their instruction. These conversations are essential for teachers to support one another in a continual examination of how they teach through a cultural lens. To create the conditions to engage in participatory inquiry, teachers first have to take several steps: build relational trust, engage in reciprocity, examine their identity and positionality, and adopt an equity stance. Let's take a closer look at each one of these steps.

Build Relational Trust

To engage in participatory inquiry, teachers must build relational trust with colleagues and students to confront bias, stereotypes, and inequitable practices. Relational trust is rooted in personal exchanges, respect, personal regard, competence, responsibility, and integrity. Relational trust creates and supports appropriate conditions to tackle inequities in schools and creates a space and the conditions in which change can occur. Relational trust is developed through interactions, conversations, tension, critical collaboration, and the demonstration of cultural competence and emotional intelligence.[10]

Engage in Reciprocity

Teachers must also engage in reciprocity: each person is responsible for contributing to the flow and knowledge of skills and for shared outcomes. There is an expectation of fair exchange of knowledge. Acknowledging that everyone has assets to bring to the table and the sharing of each person's knowledge will lead to shared, coconstructed actions that tackle inequitable practices.

Examine Identity and Positionality

Identity is how we acknowledge ourselves and informs the way we interact and navigate various contexts and information. Our identity is formed by relationships, experiences, cultural upbringing, and so on. One's identity promotes a sense of well-being, safety, and confidence in self. **Positionality** refers to the social relationships that shape the way we see and understand ourselves and dictate how we interact with one another. Our positionality shifts as we move in and navigate various contexts and interact with different people.

Take an Equity Stance

Teachers must take an equity stance. They must clearly and explicitly articulate that equity is prioritized over equality and that one's identity is prioritized over dominant norms of access and achievement. This asserts that equity is privileged in schools, and it signals a commitment to shift the discourse away from dominant norms of schooling toward narratives that place privilege on "education over schooling and power/identity over mere access and achievement."[11]

Creating these conditions to engage in participatory inquiry means that teachers need to accept accountability for what they do in classrooms. They need to remain committed to continual questioning of their beliefs and assumptions and the impact of those beliefs and assumptions on teaching practices. And, in these partnerships, they need to consider and reconsider questions that sustain the conditions for introspective inquiry into their own practices:

- **Relational trust:** How are we modeling effective communication? How are we demonstrating a sense of responsibility, accountability, and flexibility with one another?
- **Reciprocity:** How are we building on one another's knowledge and expertise? What are we both willing to commit to or shift for change to occur?
- **Identity:** How do our students' identities factor into our decision-making around classroom policies and practices? How is our identity influencing our beliefs about students, teaching, and learning?
- **Positionality:** How does our position as an educator recognize, honor, or complicate the interactions we have with students, family, and community members? In what ways are we willing to resist or disrupt the construct of our position as educators as we engage in classroom settings?
- **Equity stance:** What actions are we engaging in to dismantle the inequity and oppression that is playing out in our classrooms and school? What are we going to do to expand our knowledge and understanding of the diverse cultures in our school?

RLPs challenge people to remain open to new ways of "seeing" how they teach and how students learn, and they create intentional space for dialogue about unconscious practices that might marginalize students. Within these partnerships, teachers work to examine the historical context of school systems and coconstruct the actions they take to redesign teaching and learning for culturally diverse students. Also important, RLPs build collective efficacy and help teachers center themselves as colearners in a reciprocal dialogue—an ongoing conversation that positions everyone with knowledge and assets as someone who can enhance teaching and learning in the classroom.

Engaging in the RLP participatory inquiry process is an important step in guiding and supporting teachers in their quest to create culturally responsive teaching experiences for students. Culturally responsive teachers are continuously reassessing and examining their beliefs by explicitly identifying inequitable practices in their teaching and recognizing how their cultural identity, positionality, and bias contribute to inequity. Through participatory inquiry, they can take action that will improve students' academic, social, and emotional outcomes.

Intentional Teaching and Authentic Content

Teachers often encounter the conflict of cultural norms through language, as a fourth-grade special education teacher stated to me and my colleagues. "My teacher support staff, Mrs. Lynn, asked Donte if he finished the work that was assigned," the teacher explained. "Donte said forcefully, 'I been done did it!' She looked at him and said, 'You mean I already completed the work.' I said, 'No, he said exactly what he meant to say, and he said it correctly. He meant don't ask me again, I completed that a long time ago. You just don't understand African American language.'" Although these diverse cultural norms are often expressed in language, they come in many other forms. Therefore, intentionally shifting teaching strategies to support the cultural norms of a diverse set of students requires that teachers take the time to learn and understand the various cultural norms present in the classroom.

Teachers often ask us, How do we decide what to focus on, since our class is so culturally diverse? First, we need to be clear that most of the tensions between teachers and students lie in what's referred to as **deep culture**.[12] The educator and author Zaretta Hammond describes three levels of culture—surface, shallow, and deep. Examples of surface and shallow cultural norms include traditional games, food, dance, and music. These norms are easily seen or tangible in some way, and they tend to carry low emotional stakes. Many of these surface and shallow cultural norms are celebrated in schools.

TABLE 4.1   Examples of Deep Cultural Norms

Communication style	Tone of voice
Ideas of friendship	Decision-making
Ethics	Ideals of fairness
Gestures and facial expressions	Competition or cooperation
Rewards and privileges	Notions of time
Home language	Defining respect
Social interaction rate	Body language

Source: Wise, Tony. "Crashing into the Cultural Iceberg." Blog post from LTC Language Solutions, August 25, 2016. https://ltclanguagesolutions.com/blog/crashing-into-the-cultural-iceberg/

Deep culture, by contrast, carries high emotional stakes. It impacts how we navigate and interact with the world, and it plays a dominant role in dictating how we see others. It's the road map to our expectations of ourselves, and often our expectations of others. Teachers who are culturally responsive focus on deep culture so that they can identify and understand the real tensions between diverse students and the school. Culturally responsive teachers use a variety of instructional strategies that support and acknowledge the deep cultural norms of their diverse students, and they provide access to academic success through learning opportunities that are more authentic (see Table 4.1).

Culturally responsive teachers support these cultural norms by getting to know students. This sounds simple, but fully understanding the deep cultural beliefs, values, and norms in a classroom can reveal significant differences from the existing cultural norms of the school—and resolving those contradictions can take significant time and intentionality on the teacher's part. Teachers first need to build relational trust and mutual respect with students. However, trust and respect are culturally and contextually based, so teachers' notions of trust and respect might differ from those of their students. So, to build greater trust and respect, teachers should engage in reciprocal dialogues that seek out students' knowledge and ways of seeing the world. This fosters more clarity, encourages more input, and provides a framework in which all sides can contribute to the cocreation or redefinition of the learning space.

Also, teachers should observe and document the most common deep cultural norms that show up in their classrooms. To help in this effort, teachers can ask themselves the following questions:

- **What is their home language?** Do I have multilingual students, including those students whose home language is English but differs in significant ways from dominant/standard English? Do I have African American, American Indian, Hawaiian American, Mexican American, and other students for whom standard English is not native?
- **What are their communication patterns?** Do my students talk simultaneously when I am presenting a lesson? Do they speak out of turn and share information with neighbors without seeking my permission? There are students whose cultural norm of communication is to "simultaneously talk," or engage in cooperative overlap talk. This communication pattern signifies to others that they understand, and it shows interest and eagerness to participate.
- **Are they contextualized learners?** Do students do better when the information is authentic and connected to hands-on activities? Does the information I am providing have concrete application, and is it connected to lived experiences of the students?
- **What are their patterns of decision-making?** Do my students make decisions based on social groups and relationships?
- **What does their tone of voice indicate?** Does the tone of my students' voices rise when they are excited and passionate? Do I think that is a sign of engagement or a sign of aggression?

Teachers who create culturally responsive classroom environments use a variety of teaching strategies, but they maintain a focus on how the instructional strategy supports and acknowledges the culture of the students. As Table 4.2 shows, there are teaching strategies that teachers can use to intentionally highlight this cultural behavior and at the same time provide access to academic content.

Culturally responsive teaching requires the deliberate critique of what is presented to students. Dominant values and norms are perpetuated in schools and on social media, and they often reinforce stereotypes that hinder students from seeing themselves in positive situations or active in the dominant or mainstream culture in positive ways. Following are a few

TABLE 4.2   Culturally Responsive Teaching Strategies

Cultural Norm	What Strategy Would You Use and Why?	Dominant School Norms
Cooperative overlap talking	**What:** Allow students to participate and discuss with one another by overlapping their responses. This shows high interest in the discussion. Students are on topic, and their overlap talk is seen as a sign of engagement in the conversation. **Why:** Supports students who are sociocentric and those who make decisions that are cooperative/relational.	Raise hands Talk in turn
High movement	**What:** Intentionally have students move when discussing the work. Play music indicating when to move and discuss. **Why:** Supports students who are dynamic/rhythmic and relational.	Sit quietly in seats
Home language	**What:** Use home language in writing. Have students translate academic language to home language or home language to academic language. Read books with home language as the dominant voice. **Why:** Acknowledges that home language (this specifically includes standard English; African American, Mexican American, and Hawaiian American language; etc.) is rule-governed and is a valid form of communication. Highlights multilingualism of students.	Only have students write and respond in standard/school English (everyday language spoken in schools) or academic English (language needed for academic success)
Cooperation	**What:** Students work in pairs/groups **Why:** Supports students who are sociocentric and who make decisions based on group relationships	Competition
Contextualized learning	**What:** Provide authentic literature. Engage in oral discussions during which the context of students' experiences is brought into the story. **Why:** Supports students to engage in learning connected to self. Recognizes that context matters in how students engage and participate.	Content devoid of context

examples of how teachers in the Los Angeles area create culturally responsive teaching experiences for their students.

One middle school teacher we interviewed shared pictures of Hurricane Harvey and engaged her students in a discussion about them. She deliberately selected pictures that portrayed all genders, races, and socioeconomic backgrounds in different roles—as victims, police, and rescue workers. "I became frustrated with how many pictures I came across that had White people as the 'saviors' and people of color as the 'victims,'" she told us. "It made me wonder if this was the actuality of what is happening in Houston or if it was the media's perspective." Students worked in cooperative groups to discuss what cultural norms, values, and messages were being sent about Hurricane Harvey through pictures and social media. Students were tasked with creating counternarratives where traditional roles for women and men were challenged. During this session, students were working in groups and engaging in cooperative overlap talking with multiple people in the room. This teacher's goal was to help students understand that they must critique and question what is presented. She supported the cultural norms of her students by allowing them to use cooperative overlap talk and work in cooperative groups.

A fourth-grade teacher in an urban school district outside of Los Angeles had her students working on various aspects of writing a letter. The class was instructed to write in their home language (African American English, Mexican American English). The students were clear on what these terms meant. The teacher gave them precisely seven minutes to write one section and then asked them to translate their writing into academic language. This teacher wanted to make sure she validated the language by allowing students to write in their home language first. She then asked them to translate their letters to academic language, making sure students understood that one language was not placed in higher standing than the other. They're used for different purposes, she explained. She also used precise time with students, understanding that in her classroom, relative time is the cultural norm for her students. Switching from relative to precise time, which is the cultural norm of school and other institutions, helps students as they move through mainstream society.

A middle school math teacher was getting ready to present a lesson on ratios. She started the lesson with a story. She asked the students whether they thought a student from China, the United States, India, or Mexico scored the highest on an international math exam. Students were asked to walk to the corner corresponding to their choice and discuss their thinking behind their selection. Movement in her classroom was intentional. Having students move supported those who were dynamic. Allowing students to discuss in groups lowered the affect level for all and supported those students who were relational and cooperative. The class consisted of only Latinx and African American students. The majority of students walked over to China or India. Only one student went to Mexico. The teacher did a quick "whip around" (a nonvoluntary way to select students to respond) by asking a few in each group what they discussed and why they chose that country. She did the same for gender. Students were shocked to learn that the student who scored the highest math score on this international test was a girl from Mexico. One of the students from the back of the room yelled, "YES!" The teacher began with a story to engage her students. The story set up the context that they would use for the lesson on ratios. However, she also said that she realized that dominant norms of who is good in math were pervasive among her students of color. "We must first work on disrupting the dominant narrative that my students have bought into—that only certain people who come from certain places do well in math."

Culturally responsive teachers backward-design their instruction and content to align it with how students best learn. This includes considering the social and political context of what they are teaching. They tie their curriculum to the cultural context of their students, making it important for the student to engage and critique the dominant cultural beliefs that favor one way of knowing over the other. They present divergent viewpoints in the curriculum and connect content with the real world, making students active participants in the creation of knowledge rather than merely consumers of knowledge. And they often use technology, media, and entertainment to show competing viewpoints and cultural perspectives. Like many teachers, Melissa Ali-Bell, a fifth-grade teacher, tapped into the iconography and message of the blockbuster movie *Black Panther* to drive home lessons. Figure 4.3 shows her approach.

"Using the silhouette of (the) Black Panther is on purpose," she said. "The Black Panther movie is a huge part of Black culture and pride. The movie had a lot of symbolism in it, and we used it as a way to engage

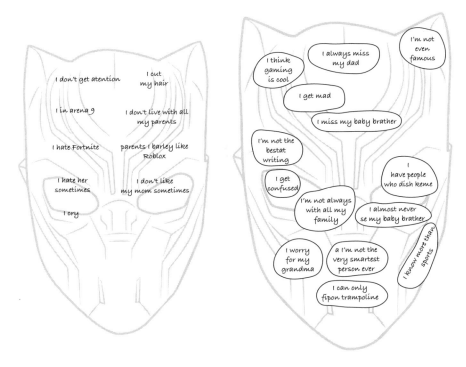

FIGURE 4.3   Black Panther Project

students in understanding their cultural knowledge of self and their social emotional state."

Ali-Bell transforms her lessons to fit the cultural context of her students, and positions their culture front and center in the learning. For a history lesson, students read *Middle Passage Together* by Charles Johnson and connected it to present issues of police brutality in the African American community. Figure 4.4 shows the resulting projects.

During another lesson, she taught division by having students compare the amount of federal spending on education versus the amount spent on defense. Students discussed what government spending says about our priorities as a country. Also, she engaged students in a science lesson around fracking. There is an area close to the school and students' homes where fracking is occurring. Students learned about fracking and discussed issues of environmental social justice, environmental racism, and the impact of fracking on their community and health.

FIGURE 4.4   Middle Passage Projects

Culturally Responsive Learning Environments

Very simply, culturally responsive learning experiences need culturally responsive classroom environments. The spaces students walk into are just as important as how and what they're taught. This means that culturally responsive teachers aim to create a classroom environment where students' culture is visible and centered as a tool for learning. Such culturally responsive classrooms display diverse people, works of art, quotes, literature, and so on. The activities that students engage in are hands-on and are often designed and created by students. Classrooms are designed so that students can easily move around the room for discussions and clearly see one

FIGURE 4.5   Posters on the Walls of a Second-Grade Classroom (left) and a Fifth-Grade Classroom (right)

another for personal connections. Traditional row seating would not be present in a culturally responsive classroom. Decorative materials on walls are colorful and comprise student work or teacher-produced posters. Pictures represent students' diverse cultural backgrounds, and icons of the past and present, including youth-oriented icons, are celebrated. Bulletin board postings are current and relevant to students' context, and libraries are properly labeled so that students can select books that directly reflect their culture, language, norms, and beliefs.

In Figure 4.5, for example, two grade-school teachers intentionally selected images that created a culturally responsive classroom environment for their African American students. These pictures represented strength, resistance, knowledge, and beauty. Also, they were pictures that young people recognized, instead of pictures of icons and heroes from the past.

Another elementary school teacher created a reading space with culturally responsive books that authentically represent the norms, language, and beliefs of her students and highlight diverse authors and illustrators (see Figure 4.6).

"It's important that students see themselves in the books they read," the teacher, NeCole Hayward, told us. "To see themselves as authors (or)

FIGURE 4.6   Culturally Responsive Reading Space

illustrators, they have to read about people who look like them, speak like them, and have led successful lives fighting oppression." This can be a challenge.

The following are examples of culturally responsive books:

- *The Autobiography of Malcolm X* as told to Alex Haley
- *The Blossoming Universe of Violet Diamond* by Brenda Woods
- *Brown Girl Dreaming* by Jacqueline Woodson
- *Feathers* by Jaqueline Woodson
- *Everlasting Nora* by Marie Miranda Cruz
- *I Am Malala* by Malala Yousafzai

We have found that virtually every culturally responsive school environment shares the following features:

- Tangible artifacts from diverse cultures
- Books that represent the cultural norms, language, and beliefs of diverse cultures
- Books that are written and illustrated by diverse authors
- Pictures and posters that represent ethnicity, gender, youth, and culture, and are relevant for students to make connections to the larger social context
- Chair and desk arrangement that allows for movement and collaboration

- Home languages represented in work posted on classroom walls
- Clear classroom expectations with coconstructed classroom norms

Creating these types of learning environments requires an intentional process that examines the classroom ecology, as well as the curriculum that is implemented and facilitated by the teacher. Culturally responsive learning environments enable authentic reflections and validation of self in what students see in classrooms and the curriculum. This incites interest, boosts engagement, and increases time on task. These learning environments seek to validate the home culture and language of students by making sure that their cultural assets are the conduit for learning. The challenge for all educators is to support the well-being of our most marginalized students. To face this challenge, it's imperative that teachers shift their teaching, content, and classroom environment toward affirming the cultures of students.

KEY TAKEAWAYS

- Being culturally responsive honors and respects the knowledge base with which each child enters school, thereby creating a learning environment where each child's gifts are acknowledged.
- Educators often unknowingly view marginalized students through a deficit lens, reacting to their culture and home language by labeling them as deficient or lacking when they disengage from a curriculum that's devoid of any connection to their daily lives. This is a false narrative, and educators must see students' culture as an asset and conduit for learning.
- Schools have continued to reproduce inequity despite major reform efforts such as No Child Left Behind and the new Common Core Standards. Major reform initiatives don't focus on changing beliefs. Creating culturally responsive learning experiences for students starts with first changing educators' mindsets and beliefs.
- Education is not neutral. Educators and students bring their culture with them in how they think and participate in teaching and learning. Engaging in participatory inquiry can support educators in understanding and engaging critically in conversations about beliefs, values, norms, race, and other factors that create tensions in classrooms.

Questions from the Field

In our conversations with teachers, very important questions regarding designing culturally responsive learning experiences arise. The following are a few that I hope are helpful in your work with students.

1. *How do I begin to examine my own cultural frames of reference?*
   Start off by asking yourself, *What inequity is taking place in my classroom?* The next question to ask is, *How is my identity (or identities) and positionality impacting the way I see the inequity, my students, and the teaching and learning?* Examining your own cultural frames can take place in RLPs. Having a partner with whom to engage in dialogue around our beliefs is important in order for us to make sure we are examining ourselves and not placing the blame on students and external causes. Remember, culturally responsive teachers first examine themselves and consistently ask, How in **my actions** do I reproduce inequity in my classroom?

2. *How do I know what deep cultural norms are present in my classroom? How will I address those norms to create a culturally responsive teaching environment?*
   Begin by observing and documenting what cultural norms are exhibited by the students in your classroom (Table 4.1). Once you determine, for example, their communication style, whether they are sociocentric/relational learners, whether they overlap talk, and so on, you can adjust your instructional style to support that cultural element. You then address those cultural norms by making sure that your instructional strategies allow for students to overlap talk, allow the use of home language in drafts or oral presentations, and make sure movement is incorporated into how you ask students to engage in the lesson.

3. *Where do I find culturally responsive lessons and guidelines to help me understand how to support standard or nondominant English learners such as African American and Mexican American language speakers?*
   The Los Angeles Unified School District's Academic English Mastery Program offers a wealth of knowledge. This department is

dedicated to standard English learners; it has linguistic screeners and lesson plans for all grade levels and content areas. Also, on the department's site are professional development resources and culturally responsive tools and books. The Center for Culturally Responsive Teaching and Learning is also a great resource and provides videos as well as a workbook to guide teachers on their journey to becoming more culturally responsive.

Recommended Resources

Institute for Cultural Sustainability and Educational Equity, UCLA Center X (https://centerx.gseis.ucla.edu/icsee/). This institute supports educators in transforming their schools into more effective spaces for educating culturally diverse students by developing their knowledge base around teaching and learning that is equity focused and culturally relevant, responsive, and sustaining. It provides professional learning opportunities addressing culturally responsive and relevant pedagogy and reciprocal learning partnerships for equity.

Los Angeles Unified School District Academic English Mastery Program (https://achieve.lausd.net/AEMP). This comprehensive, research-based program supports teachers in their ability to address the language and literacy needs of African American, Mexican American, Hawaiian American, and American Indian students for whom dominant/standard English is not native. The program has professional development, instructional strategies, and lesson plans available to facilitate the language learning of culturally diverse students.

Center for Culturally Responsive Teaching and Learning (CCRTL) (https://www.culturallyresponsive.org/). Based in Los Angeles, CCRTL provides literature, videos, professional development, and teacher resources on implementing culturally responsive pedagogy.

New York Metropolitan Center for Research on Equity and the Transformation of Schools (www.napequity.org). This organization promotes equity and school improvement through research, programs, evaluation, and professional assistance to agencies serving the most vulnerable populations. It created the "Culturally Responsive Scorecard." This is a good starting place for teachers to determine how culturally responsive their curriculum is currently.

National Alliance for Partnerships in Equity. This organization offers professional development and resources on culturally responsive pedagogy.

5

Promoting Critical Wellness with Young Learners

ANDRÉA C. MINKOFF

Teachers are often the first adults outside the family to influence young children. There has been extensive research over the years about how important high-quality education is in early childhood development, both in students' early years and for the rest of their lives.[1] Although many educators and researchers have studied various ways to improve early interventions, less work has focused on how to effectively prepare early childhood educators as they teach young kids about diversity and identity. Those of us who have been around children know that those issues are incredibly important and that kids come to school with rapidly developing ideas about socially constructed categories, such as race, class, and gender.[2] It's critical that we understand how to prepare and support teachers so that they can engage in these topics in meaningful ways in the classroom—our goal is always for every child to thrive.

The world is changing rapidly; demographic shifts and migration flows around the country mean that kids today are being educated in increasingly multicultural settings.[3] Research suggests that some teachers are not as prepared as they should be—in fact, many suffer from **deficit thinking** about nondominant students and their communities, meaning that unquestioned assumptions and stereotypes lead educators to assume that students of differing backgrounds have a deficit that teachers need to fix.[4] Rather than proactively and positively supporting the strengths inherent in diversity- and identity-related attributes, educators caught in deficit thinking set out to repair what they see as disadvantage. That's why it's especially important that early childhood educators enter the classroom with skills they can use to educate and support all students.

According to Howard and Milner, teachers need three types of knowledge to make classroom spaces meaningful and relevant to students:[5]

1. Subject matter knowledge
2. Pedagogical content knowledge
3. Racial and cultural knowledge

This chapter focuses on the last of these knowledge categories: the development of racial and cultural knowledge, including the critical self-reflection in which all teachers need to engage in order to understand their own **implicit social biases**. (You will sometimes encounter the term *unconscious bias* in place of implicit bias—the terms can be used interchangeably.) As race and culture continue to shift in schools, preservice and in-service teacher education must deal with these issues so that teachers are prepared to work effectively with young learners who bring a variety of identities and understandings of the world to the classroom.

Development of Racial Attitudes and Racial-Ethnic Socialization

It's a common misconception that children do not see race, but research shows that children as young as six months old can tell the differences between both race and gender.[6] As children grow, their racial awareness develops as well; children as young as three to five years old can express explicit racial biases and preferences.[7] Children reveal they have these biases and preferences through the way they identify themselves and others ("I'm like this and you're not") or by whom they include or exclude when they play ("I don't want to play with you because you're different from me"). Because children develop and act on this keen awareness at such an early age, it's crucial to make sure they have plenty of opportunities to discuss race. However, parents too often remain silent on issues of race with their children, especially at young ages.[8] Parents of children of color are more likely to socialize their children around issues of race than their White counterparts.[9] At the same time, findings suggest that even parents of color resist engaging in conversations about racial discrimination with preschool-age children, even though they might recognize the importance of their children's having this knowledge and preparation.[10] Parents are much more likely to talk about race as their children become teenagers.[11] But these conversations cannot—and should not—be delayed. Young kids develop racial attitudes rapidly. The fact that parents are often silent about these issues means it's even more important for children to have teachers who critically engage their students in conversations about race, racism, and racial identity from an early age.

More often than not, parents may decide that being **color-mute**— suppressing any talk about race—is the better way to help their kids because they're afraid that discussing race is more likely to make their kids racist.[12] In addition to not initiating racial discussions with children in the first place, parents generally don't speak up when their kids say things that reveal racial biases, either.[13] Parents might mean well when they don't talk about race, thinking that they're trying to avoid nurturing racial bias in their children—but instead, the opposite occurs. Experts have shown that White parents who don't talk about differences in race or ethnicity—parents who are trying to help their kids be "color-blind"—still have children who grow up with pro-White racial preferences and who use stereotypes to talk about other kids' traits.[14]

Fortunately, this can be reversed, and children who are given opportunities to engage in explicit conversations about race can change. One study found that White children who were exposed to school lessons about historical racism demonstrated more positive and less negative views of their African American counterparts.[15] That study also showed that both White and Black students exposed to antiracist lessons also valued racial fairness more than children who did not receive such lessons. This is why early childhood educators can play such an important role. Engaging children in explicit conversations about race and racism can improve race relations in the United States and create a more harmonious society. Parents might not always be willing to change their positions—research shows that many parents want to keep being color-mute even when they learn that discussing race is a better strategy.[16] The classroom then becomes an even more important alternative space to engage issues of race for students.

Shifting Demographics and the Demographic Divide

This issue grows even more critical when we look at the shifting demographics in the student population (see chapter 1). As the nation becomes more diverse, public schools in urban areas are more likely to be attended by African American, Asian/Pacific Islander, and Latinx students than White students.[17] Those same schools are also more likely to be staffed by White women than by women or men of color.[18] This demographic difference between students and teachers in our nation's schools underscores the importance of racial difference and racial identity.

To be clear, good teachers do not have to share the same racial identity as the students they teach. According to Tenore, Dunn, Laughter, and Milner, "Teachers from any ethnic, cultural, or racial background can be successful with any group of students when the teachers possess (or have the drive and commitment to acquire) the knowledge, attitudes, dispositions, and beliefs necessary to teach all students well."[19] Developing a strong sense of racial identity is a vital first step in helping all students thrive.

One way that teacher education programs and in-service teacher professional development can help prepare teachers to work with diverse students and facilitate critical wellness is by supporting the development of racial identity. Most preservice teachers grew up in monoracial communities and had little to no interaction with members of different racial backgrounds.[20] This happens because increased diversity is often associated with increased segregation. These teachers may endorse or unintentionally harbor stereotypical and negative thoughts about communities of color that they learned in college or through their home cultures.[21] In addition to possibly holding negative stereotypes about the students they teach, many preservice teachers don't have enough information about their own **social identities*** in today's racialized society.

This lack of information can significantly inhibit the effectiveness of early childhood educators, as evidenced by the growing body of research that shows how teachers' racial stereotypes can have significant consequences for even very young children. Recent data on preschool expulsions show that Black boys are 3.6 times more likely to be pushed out of school at a young age than their White counterparts.[22] A study by Gilliam, Maupin, Reyes, Accavitti, and Shic demonstrates what teacher bias against young Black boys in preschool settings looks like: early childhood educators

---

* As defined by Derman-Sparks and Edwards in *Anti-Bias Education for Young Children and Ourselves* (National Association for the Education of Young Children, 2010), social identities are "the significant group categorizations assigned to use by the society in which we grow up and live and which we share with many others. These include our racial, ethnic/cultural, gender, and religious identities, as well as economic class, geographic identities, and so on" (p. 12).

were shown video clips of four preschool children (a Black boy, a Black girl, a White boy, and a White girl) and were told to look for "challenging behaviors." They looked at the Black boy 42 percent of the time—more than any of the other children.[23]

This teacher bias also impacts teacher–parent communication. Teachers are more likely to contact Black and Latinx parents about behavioral problems and less likely to reach out to immigrant Latinx and Asian families to share student accomplishments.[24] This trend is devastating not only for the child on the receiving end of such treatment but also for other students in the classroom who are learning how to treat their fellow students. Derman-Sparks and Ramsey make it clear: a "key influence on children's ideas about others comes from the ideas and messages surrounding them."[25] Much of the research over the last few decades about how we pass on ideas of race, ethnicity, and gender to children has focused on parents and what happens in the home.[26] But there is increasing evidence that the implicit bias of teachers can have a direct impact on the implicit prejudice of students.[27] Teachers must become more conscious and more reflective about their own racial identities and implicit biases so that they can create healthier learning environments for all young children.

Engaging Racial Identity among Early Childhood Professionals

The first step toward becoming the kind of teacher who can effectively teach students from all backgrounds is to understand the power and significance of one's own identity. Self-reflection and empathy—the very traits that make teachers more effective practitioners—are also necessary to engage in identity development and racial awareness. As Carter and Goodwin put it, "the racial identity levels of educators themselves influence how they perceive and interact with children of color."[28] These levels can also predict how well a teacher will accept diversity in the prekindergarten classroom.[29] In their work, Sanders and Downer noticed a concerning trend: pre-kindergarten teachers were more likely to be White, and White pre-kindergarten teachers were less likely to accept diversity in their classrooms.[30]

But this is a trend that can be fixed. Han, West-Olatunji, and Thomas analyzed the cultural competence of White early childhood educators by looking at how much they had thought about their own racial identities.[31] The results were encouraging: teachers who never thought of or questioned their own racial identity—that is, those who fit into the first level of Helms's White racial identity development model**—were more likely to endorse "color-blind" teaching in their classroom and downplay the importance of multicultural education with preschoolers. However, the participants who had done some of the self-reflective work and who had moved further in their White racial identity development were more likely to recognize their racial privilege. Having critically reflected on their own identities and made conscious attempts to eliminate their own implicit biases, these teachers could have a deeper and more positive influence on all their students.

Implicit Bias and Intergroup Contact: Teachers and Young Learners

Implicit bias (see chapter 3) refers to attitudes that affect our understanding, choices, and actions in unconscious ways.[32] Research on implicit **social cognition**—how people process, understand, and engage with other people and social situations—reveals that adults' implicit biases are reflected visibly in children at a young age, even as young as early infancy.[33] By the time children are six years old, they exhibit levels of implicit bias on par with adults.[34] This early emergence of implicit bias appears especially prominent in White children, in whom it appears at a young age and remains stable as they transition into adulthood.[35]

Fortunately, studies also show that implicit bias among adults can be reduced,[36] and that these biases are most changeable after they are formed.[37] This opens up the hope and possibility that we can shape healthier racial attitudes in teachers and young children alike. For this reason, the rest of this chapter offers concrete suggestions for practitioners to do the hard work of reflecting on their identity and reducing their bias so that they can facilitate critical wellness for themselves and the young learners they serve.

Recommendations for Practice

Teachers should critically reflect on their own identity development and the origins of their own childhood socialization around race, and then create opportunities for children to do the same.

**Helms's White racial identity development model is a model of racial identity development for individuals who identify as White. The model progresses through six stages, during which an individual moves from endorsing color-blind to anti-racist ideologies.

When doing in-service professional development with educators, we ask teachers to reflect critically on their own **implicit racial conditioning**—what and how they learned about race. After giving participants some time to individually process the messages they received about people like them and people who were different from them as children, they then talk to one another about similarities and differences in their upbringings. They also consider how the messages and narratives they learned contributed to both their reflective and automatic preferences.

This practice of self-reflection and sharing is critical for helping teachers understand themselves—a prerequisite for understanding the experiences of a diverse set of students.[38] Although opportunities to critically reflect on one's experiences with identity and socialization have become increasingly common in preservice teacher education,[39] it is important that educators continue to practice this type of reflection once they enter the profession. This is particularly vital for teachers who work with young students and use anti-bias multicultural materials that oblige them to learn and grow with their pupils.[40]

Teachers need to create similar opportunities for students to reflect on and share aspects of their own identity as well. When teachers use responsive classroom practices that humanize their students, they build a sense of classroom community and validate young learners, but they also reduce biases. Some strategies that teachers can use include individuation, perspective taking, and creating opportunities for positive contact.[41] Thus teachers can help students resist unconscious biases by creating opportunities for students to see their peers for the qualities that make them unique instead of letting group stereotypes guide thinking (individuation), understand other students' points of view (perspective taking), and experience more moments of positive contact with a diverse set of peers. In the early childhood classroom, this can take the form of having students complete "All About Me" posters and share their stories with their teachers and peers throughout the year. By encouraging students to talk about where they are coming from, teachers not only learn more about the "funds of knowledge"[42] that students bring to school but also learn more about their students as individuals (particularly in the context of bias). Seeing each student as an individual can break down the power of stereotypes that might drive deficit thinking. In addition, letting students be individuals can facilitate shared perspective-taking among teachers and young learners. Research indicates that such perspective-taking is critical for developing empathy and closeness, which disrupts the types of automatic thinking and behavior that arise from negative stereotypes.[43] Thus students and teachers can engage in parallel processes that support bias reduction and healthier intergroup relations in the classroom.

Teachers should work to intentionally identify and eliminate bias in their classrooms.

As the popular expression says, "One can't be what one can't see." We find this holds true when it comes to the way that mentors and role models shape implicit attitudes. A classic study on children's racial and gender attitudes brings this expression to life: when school-age children were asked to draw a scientist, 92 percent of boys and 86 percent of girls drew a male scientist, and almost 99 percent of children drew the scientist as White.[44] This has important implications when we consider what children see (and don't see) in the context of the early childhood classroom. Sometimes even simple changes, such as what appears on a computer screen saver,[45] can produce large shifts because they enable our brains to build new associations that challenge the stereotypical concepts to which we're exposed in daily life.

Banaji and Greenwald refer to these shifts as **elastic changes**.[46] They acknowledge that these shifts can be significant, but, like a piece of elastic that stretches and then returns to its initial shape, these concepts can and will return to previous forms unless consistent exposure takes place. The data on consistent exposure, however, is encouraging. Research with college-age students indicates that the more they are exposed to counter-stereotypical images, the weaker their gendered associations, such as when they think of women and math or women as leaders.[47]

When working with teachers, it is important to ask them to reflect on what their classroom environment looks like and how it might shape the ways in which young learners view the world. According to Derman-Sparks and Edwards,

> The toys, materials, and equipment you put out for children; the posters, the pictures, and art objects you hang on the wall; and the types

of furniture and how you arrange them all influence what children learn. An environment rich in anti-bias materials invites exploration and discovery and supports children's play and conversations in both emergent and planned activities. It alerts children to which issues the teacher thinks are important and unimportant. What children do *not* see in the classroom teaches children as much as what they do see.[48]

Given the formative role the classroom environment plays in development, teachers need to constantly assess the visual surroundings of their schools and spaces.[49] How are dynamics of visibility and invisibility functioning in the classroom? What books are in the classroom library? What stories are being told? Do visuals represent different types of people engaging in different types of activities? Is care being taken to make sure that there are no token images? Considering that implicit biases are like bad habits, research does show that they can change with intention, attention, and time.[50] Taking the time to "de-bias" a classroom environment creates a more inclusive learning community, while validating and affirming the many types of young learners. Teachers play a pivotal role in building healthier associations, both in themselves and in children, that contribute to educational wellness.

Teachers should work to develop relationships with colleagues who are also committed to promoting critical wellness among their students.
Because the brain is a social organ[51] and bias is a consequence of human cognition,[52] working with other colleagues who are likewise committed to reducing the impact of bias can be transformative. According to Diane Finnerty, self-change is important, but if we don't work to shift systems, we are doing little to truly develop critical wellness for our students.[53] Finnerty recommends engaging in critical reflective practice to empower teachers to function as change agents in their community and profession. Specifically, teachers can either observe one another's lessons (or videotape their lessons if in-person visits to other classrooms aren't possible) or ask colleagues to assess their work for micro and macro forms of bias. Such support is common during student teaching and during teacher induction programs, but we can extend this type of field support beyond general pedagogical support to focus on issues of identity and

bias as well. Separately, teachers can form reading groups that help them think more critically about issues of identity and bias in their work as educators. (For helpful materials, see the recommended resources at the end of the chapter.)

KEY TAKEAWAYS

- The field of early childhood education is uniquely positioned to create effective learning environments for young children, providing them the anti-bias curricula they need and the critical teachers who help empower them as they work to make sense of the rapidly diversifying world in which they live. According to Winkler, "if anti-bias education exists in school curricula at all, it tends to be too little, too late."[54]

- We need to clearly recognize the important social position of teachers of young learners in today's world. Given that young children quickly develop racial attitudes and ideas, it becomes ever more important that their teachers come to the classroom prepared to teach socially just ideas about race, racism, power, and privilege in ways that promote healthy racial attitudes and combat racially problematic beliefs. Young children need and deserve empathetic adults who can support them as they establish the foundation that helps them thrive and succeed in a diverse world.

- For early childhood educators to do this effectively, they must be willing to engage in a journey of critical self-reflection about their own sense of identity and their implicit biases. Fortunately, with attention and time, biased attitudes can be reduced and identity can be deepened. We can do this through critical self-reflection, intentionally constructing learning environments that are visually reflective of diversity, and working collaboratively with other colleagues committed to this journey. Such practices are crucial for promoting critical wellness in early childhood education, where students form ideas about peers, cross-cultural interactions, and differences.

Questions from the Field

In our conversations with teachers, very important questions regarding critical wellness arise. The following are a few that I hope are helpful in your work with students.

1. *But I don't mean to act in ways that are considered racist. Shouldn't that be enough?*

   I take a hard line with this one: if educators are acting in ways that are intentionally biased, they should not be working with youth. That being said, it is important to consider the difference between intention and impact. I can step on someone's foot, and I may not mean to do it, but that doesn't mean that my actions didn't cause pain. The impact is still felt, even if the intention to cause harm was not there. As stated explicitly by Pine and Hilliard, "Prejudice, discrimination, and racism do not require intention."[55] Recognizing this is an important first step. Further, it is also imperative to recognize that we all harbor biases as a function of coming of age in a racist society, and because of that socialization, we may act in ways that we did not intend to. Tatum offers us an analogy that helps us recognize how this happens:

   > Cultural racism—the cultural images and messages that affirm the assumed superiority of Whites and the assumed inferiority of people of color—is like smog in the air. Sometimes it is so thick it is visible, other times it is less apparent, but always, day in and day out, we are breathing it in. None of us would introduce ourselves as "smog breathers" (and most of us don't want to be described as prejudiced), but if we live in a smoggy place, how can we avoid breathing the air? If we live in an environment in which we are bombarded with stereotypical images in the media, are frequently exposed to the ethnic jokes of friends and family members, and are rarely informed of the accomplishments of oppressed groups, we will develop the negative categorizations of those groups that form the basis of prejudice.[56]

Given that we have been breathing in the smog of cultural racism for years, it is very likely that we unintentionally act in ways that perpetuate it. With mindfulness, and some of the strategies discussed in this chapter, we can bring what was once unconscious and unintentional to the forefront of our minds and work to be better for the students and communities we serve.

2. *I noticed that a lot of the research you shared with us used Black and White participants. This doesn't mirror our school demographics. Does that mean that it doesn't apply to us?*

This is an excellent question and one that points to an ongoing concern with research and theory on race, racism, and racialization in the United States: the issue of the Black/White binary. As Gonzalez-Sobrino and Goss assert, "The importance and uniqueness of the experiences of black people, as well as the continued forms of anti-black discrimination, still holds true. Yet, there is a profound need to explore the experiences of new (and old) racial and ethnic groups that transgress the colour binary."[57] As research expands to be more inclusive, it is important to keep in mind that the cognitive mechanisms associated with developing and eliminating bias hold true across different groups. Although the qualitative nature of the consequences and manifestations of bias will vary from context to context, the strategies shared in this chapter can be used effectively in a variety of different settings. I encourage teachers to reflect on their context and take stock of where they see the impact of bias. For example, at a school with a predominantly Latinx population, how does bias manifest? Skin color? Language? Immigration? Through self-study, teachers can reflect on the demographics of the students and families they serve and consider the ways that they can adopt these strategies and tailor them to respond to the needs of the students and families with whom they work.

Recommended Resources

Banaji, M. R., & Greenwald, A. G. (2013). *Blindspot: Hidden biases of good people*. New York, NY: Random House. This book gives a wonderful overview of the ways in which implicit bias functions, as well as a history of the research on implicit bias, with specific attention paid to the Implicit Association Test. In addition to a thorough review of the research on implicit bias, this book also details ways to reduce bias.

Derman-Sparks, L., & Edwards, J. O. (2010). *Anti-bias education for young children and ourselves*. Washington, DC: NAEYC. This is a must-have book for every early childhood educator. In this classic text, Derman-Sparks and Edwards define and explore anti-bias education for young learners, and discuss strategies for engaging children around issues of identity, including, but not limited to, race, class, gender, ability, and family structure.

Derman-Sparks, L., & Ramsey, P. G. (2011). *What if all the kids are white? Anti-bias multicultural education with young children and families*. New York, NY: Teachers College Press. Extending these authors' previous contributions, this text explores what it means to do this work in learning spaces that lack racial diversity. Specific attention is paid to how to engage these topics with White children and families, and the book also offers insight into White identity development and processes connected to facilitating care and activism.

6

Creating a College-Going Culture

JONLI D. TUNSTALL

S tudents of color access higher education opportunities at rates far lower than their White and Asian peers, largely because they face restricted access to the resources at the K–12 level that support college preparation and college going. According to 2017 data from the National Center for Education Statistics, just 36 percent of African American and Latinx students enroll in a four-year university, compared with 41 percent for White and 65 percent for Asian students.[1] Low-income and racially diverse students more often attend schools with higher levels of segregation, lower levels of teacher quality, and fewer resources to support teachers and staff. Students from marginalized populations compete on an inequitable playing field.

The idea that students of color from disadvantaged backgrounds cannot compete at the same level is erroneous. Although individual experiences and home environments influence student achievement, research shows that school environments play an increasingly vital role in preparedness for college and career attainment. So how do we begin to create a stronger pipeline from kindergarten to twelfth grade, and beyond into higher education? How do we increase the level of access that historically marginalized populations have to institutions of higher learning? How do we create a school-wide college-going culture?

As educators, we have done little to provide satisfactory answers to children who ask the obvious questions: "If I don't like school now, why would I go to more school? If school is boring and I don't see myself reflected in what I'm learning and its relevance to my life, then why go for more?" We readily note that more education leads to higher earning power in the US labor market. We might talk about the greater options and flexibility these educational skills can afford a worker over the course of his or her career. Yet we fail to put in the detailed, at times uncomfortable and difficult work to answer those questions in ways to which students can fully relate and that enable them to see the relevance of what they are learning now to who they are. Creating a true college-going culture means that the possibility of attending college is ingrained in the very fabric of the school, the curriculum, and how teachers operate their classrooms and interact with their students. It means preparing young minds not only for entry into a university environment but also for persistence and success once they enroll. College preparation is very different for students of color, because it also means being equipped with the tools to persist through a potentially culturally isolating and a sometimes even hostile racial environment. It involves both academic and social preparation in ways that belie the seeming simplicity of the idea of a "college-going culture."

Important components of a college-going culture include equipping students not only with the academic skills and knowledge for college success but also with the soft skills that we do not always think about when we talk about students being "college-ready." Schools with a strong college-going culture also employ staff who help all students access rigorous courses,[2] and include a curriculum that promotes student achievement[3] and equips them with the time management, study, critical thinking, and other academic behaviors and skills they need for college.[4] Students in urban schools often experience a watered-down curriculum in primary school, and only a small segment of the school population has access to the advanced classes necessary for college entry.

Classrooms must instead foster an environment where students are able to express opinions and to debate and critique ideas with which they might disagree. Students must have the opportunity to infuse their personal experiences into assignments and discussions, and have the confidence and resilience to accept thoughtful critique and embrace the experiences of others. Too few primary and secondary curricula are designed to build these sorts of skills—to engage with students' lives and embrace the individual diversity they bring to the classroom. Often students are relegated to the cycle of reading, copying, and spewing back what they heard from the teacher or the book, absent any real analysis or critique.

Teachers who effectively engage and empower students of color talk regularly about the number of opportunities students have to incorporate their own experiences and their own voice in the classroom. Whether through the writing they do or the discussions in class, bringing the students' home or community environment into that room creates a space in which everyone can contribute. The effects this has on students' academic self-concepts and achievement are qualitatively palpable and quantitatively measurable, particularly when districts put these strategies to work not just in high schools but in middle and elementary schools as well. Habits—time management, impulse control, planning and prioritizing, organization, and study habits—are formed in middle school and last throughout adulthood. If we are waiting for high school, we are too late. By then, students have established hard-to-break habits. More often than not, they have been tracked into highly gifted routes or saddled with low expectations, whether in formal programs or teacher perceptions. As early as first grade, students can internalize how others see them in an academic space, and that starts to become ingrained in how they then perform and even see themselves. So how do we nurture students' academic self-concept early on, and not just wait until their junior year in high school to say, "Let's start thinking about what's next" and "You can do it" when they have been hearing for so many years that they can't.

We do not assume that all students will go or want to go to college. Establishing a district-wide college-going culture is not about convincing every child to try for the Ivy League; it is about making that a realistic option for those who dream of doing so. It is about unveiling the sometimes hidden curriculum around college access that is only available to some districts, some schools, some small learning communities, some students. It is about shifting to a culture that opens possibilities to all, while remaining aware of the reality that creating that sort of environment for everyone is no easy task.

What's Missing in Many Schools

The entirety of this book calls for educators to radically rethink how we look at students, their situations, and their communities, and to create more culturally and socially responsive learning environments. Few teachers, however, are trained to integrate a student's outside individual and community experiences into the curriculum and classroom environment. Yet research shows that employing a **culturally relevant pedagogy**—one that engages the individual growth of students, celebrates their culture, honors the culture of others, and analyzes real-world issues—produces significantly greater outcomes for students of color.[5] This three-pronged consideration of academic success, cultural competency, and sociopolitical consciousness increases the relevance of lessons for the students learning them. Ladson-Billings's pivotal work calls for culturally relevant teachers to utilize students' culture as a vehicle for learning.[6] Simply put, when students see themselves reflected in the curriculum, they engage more in the learning process.

The academic success considerations might require a shift in how a teacher defines student achievement. In my work with teachers, having them talk about the different ways they define academic success and encourage students' individual growth reveals an array of examples of effective measurements. Instead of a child's success being measured solely in terms of maintaining or improving test scores, it might also take into consideration the way the student's classroom participation and engagement with other students flourished from the start to the end of a semester. It might include a student's ability to connect what he or she learned in October to a lesson in January. One middle school teacher in a New York public school described "good faith" assignments that enable students to be the expert by having them write narratives about themselves—an assignment for which every student earns an A. In the first week of every school year, he would learn about his individual students through these narratives and could then build off of that week to week, incorporating relevant ideas and media (e.g., music and video) into lessons and class discussions. These alternative but still rigorous measures of achievement—assessing growth from one month to the next, for instance—enhance academic confidence and success and enable teachers to learn about each of their students.

Of course, making education culturally relevant also requires that teachers learn about their students' culture and about the community in which most of their students live—and then reflect that understanding in how they engage with students and craft their lesson plans. But in addition to that, they have to create an in-school environment that establishes the relevance of their students' experiences while also putting these experiences in the context of other diverse experiences. This helps build a skill set for college, where students must engage in a culture outside their own. In many cases, this involves bringing the real world into the classroom space, requiring that teachers create environments for students to engage with these often-fraught issues, while also feeling comfortable leading those discussions.

Establishing these sorts of classroom environments also shifts us from a **pedagogy of poverty** to a **pedagogy of plenty**.[7] Rather than the traditional rote styles of K–12 learning, which centered more on memorization, homework with little feedback, and simply moving students on from here, a pedagogy of plenty thinks beyond just one particular classroom space and students knowing just one particular answer. It creates a place for students to broaden their learning experience and allows teachers to connect a much wider variety of lesson points for students. I often think about one seventh-grade teacher, Mr. Quest, who loved figuring out how to incorporate culture and the surrounding world into the classroom space, and even challenging school norms when doing so. There was nothing he was afraid to use as a learning tool. He had his students critique the Pledge of Allegiance and gave his students shared power in the classroom space and a platform to understand what the pledge means for their cultural environment. Quest said, "I told them it was optional. There was a school rule around [reciting] it, but I taught it breeds too much nationalism, which can be dangerous. However, if they wanted to pledge, I told them it was fine." It does not take too much imagination to see how this begins to create more-engaged learners able to critique the world around them.

Simply put, what these teachers demonstrate is care. Thus a college-going culture intentionally engages a culturally diverse student body but also involves caring individuals. Although this might seem trite and too simplistic to some, education research on resilient students found that a favorite teacher who served as more than just an instructor for academic skills was among the most frequently encountered positive role models outside of the family circle.[8] A caring relationship with a teacher gives youth further motivation for wanting to succeed.[9] **Resilience theory** illustrates just how significantly a caring individual with high expectations in students' lives can help them persist and achieve. This need not require an adult's full immersion in every aspect of a child's life. In fact, research shows that students who experience such involvement in at least one facet produce better academic outcomes.[10] When students have at least one person in their life who cares about them and has high expectations of them—perhaps a counselor or a church member who helps them work through issues of instability in a foster home—that becomes the turning point for their self-image, confidence, and academic trajectory. This kind of relationship builds internal resilience, exhibits care, and creates a support network where one might not be present otherwise.

Years ago, I interviewed a student, the oldest of eleven kids in an emotionally and verbally abusive home environment. In middle school, she already had to care for her younger siblings, and her mother did not care whether or not she attended school. Yet when she told me of her experience from kindergarten through sixth grade, she talked about the role of . individuals who cared for her along her journey. A teacher noticed that she was not coming to school and got the district's permission to pick her up. Other administrators noticed how well she was doing in certain subjects and slotted her into higher-level classes. Leaders in college-prep programs made allowances for her given her lack of familial involvement and gave her access to college classes and college-prep information. And someone at her church helped her fill out her college application and complete the FAFSA, and moved her into her college dorm. She was fortunate to find such a series of concerned and caring adults, yet none of those adults had to make extraordinary interventions across multiple facets of her life. Collectively, with relatively modest involvement, they contributed to her own resiliency, enabling her to excel.

Schools and educators must build the kinds of environments that foster more of these types of resiliency-building engagements that provide culturally relevant classroom experiences and establish a pervasive college-going culture.

Key Components for Creating a College-Going Culture

The educational environments from which college-bound students readily emerge tend to display similar characteristics. They identify the strengths students have and build on them. They incorporate rigor in the classroom and push students to achieve. And, particularly in under-resourced, disadvantaged communities, they incorporate culturally proficient practices, so that students see themselves in the curriculum. Establishing all of these elements has become increasingly difficult in a system focused on achievement on standardized tests. The race to prepare young people for tests leaves teachers little capacity to learn about their students' culture and community and prepare a lesson that incorporates those notions. Hence, although the long-term effects of these strategies are great, they often require additional time, skills, and training that are not available to teachers. Yet focusing on a handful of high-level components—curriculum; school culture and teacher beliefs; school events, environment, and exposure; and educational resources—can provide a few touchpoints where educators can start building an effective college-going culture.

Curriculum

A culturally relevant curriculum that honors students' experiences and brings their voice to the classroom enables them to engage in, see the relevance of, and connect with what they are learning. Previous chapters illustrate the importance of racially affirming and culturally supportive learning spaces to educational wellness. This same concept is the underpinning of creating a college-going culture. Educators at all levels must develop racial awareness and cultural competence to effectively engage students in the learning process and to build their desire to continue in their educational journey. This brings with it the challenge to discover ways to blend students' culture with another diverse cultural experience to provide both relevance of the known and discovery of the new.

In my conversations with teachers in urban schools about how they develop and use culturally relevant curriculum, they share that this extends beyond how students are reflected in reading material and rote assignments; it also taps into youth culture and engaging students where they are. Some teachers incorporate social media platforms, and others use more music, GIFs, or video in the classroom. Teachers who espouse a culturally relevant curriculum also try to incorporate real-world events in their classroom space. This can include discussions and assignments on the role that government and community institutions play in students' everyday lives, on the impact of unjust immigration reform on their communities, or on topics ranging from climate change in science class to the historical analysis of protests in concert with upcoming teachers' strikes.

How does a teacher from a White, middle-class family overcome the awkwardness of talking to students of color about police shootings of unarmed African American teens or the challenges faced by undocumented immigrants? Unfortunately, what we find at times is how uncomfortable educators are in discussing race and racism in schools. Students often are the first to know about what is going on around the world because they are on social media platforms that provide them with in-the-moment accounts of what is happening in their local, national, and even international environments. So although teachers are reticent to broach social issues in class, students are primed to participate in classroom discussions on contemporary world issues that could be guided and facilitated by informed teachers. Are we afraid to engage in world issues because we feel as though class is not the place for it? Incorporating such issues may be easier for our history teachers and our English teachers, but do we see a cultural relevance for our science and math teachers as well? This might require that teachers change their lesson plans from one semester to the next, but the relevance of the curriculum and what it reflects is a primary starting point for a college-going culture.

School Culture and Teacher Beliefs

School culture involves the way teachers, administrators, and school staff collectively influence the functioning of the school and extends to how classroom practices and teacher–student interactions impact students' performance, self-efficacy, and academic self-concept. A culture of care and teachers' belief in each student's ability to access college enhance readiness for higher education. A culture of care involves a variety of individuals on the same school campus. For some students it is an administrator, for others it is their teacher, but students know when folks do not care about them. They know when their teacher is disengaged. They know when it is just a paycheck for their teacher. They know when their teacher is only going to be there for a year. Even when teachers and administrators pass them through, they can spot the spaces where care is present or missing.

Students can also sense the sort of belief that cripples their interest or shores up their resilience. When we talk to students outside the classroom and compare those conversations with our teacher interviews, the students almost invariably pinpoint their teacher's opinion of them. So teachers might have those conversations at home or with their colleagues at work, and use those discussions, consciously or subconsciously, to identify the students they need to invest in rather than give up on in their class. That sort of belief shows up every day in what students choose to care about and what they choose to ignore.

So even though we have to talk about the hard academic skills and the curriculum, we also need to think about the role that care and belief play in the ways teachers and administrators engage with students. Whether they are offering a high five or a simple word of affirmation when talking with a struggling student, educators need to think about how to create a classroom environment that makes students believe in themselves and to create an overall school environment that demonstrates care.

School Environment, Events, and Exposure

In addition to considerations about curriculum and building a culture of care and belief, the school's physical environment, the events that take place on campus, and the ideas to which students are exposed play a vital role in building a college-going culture. From hallways that affirm student potential to themed classrooms, a student's surroundings need to reflect consistent exposure to college opportunities. Much about creating a college culture can seem overwhelming, but the small things add up, too, such as themed classrooms decorated or designed to correspond to a particular college or university. For example, a University of Michigan classroom with school banners and colors seeds a student's imagination of college life in Ann Arbor. As students switch classrooms, they learn about a different school and are exposed to a variety of options every day and every new school year. Even something as seemingly simple as altering the physical environment exposes students to new and different experiences, priming them and opening their imagination to different opportunities.

Resources

To a great degree, the resources a school provides very much overlap with the environment, events, and exposure just described. I list it separately here because the concept of resources adds an element of external opportunities, experiences, and constituencies. This might include college and university visits not just during a student's senior year but throughout K–12 education. This begins to give students a sense of a college environment and fosters direct engagement between colleges, college students, and the next generation of scholars coming their way. Teachers can also invite friends and people from the surrounding community to present a wide variety of career options for students. Doctors, lawyers, and businesspeople are often the extent of career options that students imagine, unaware of the array of professional and vocational options available to them. Exposure to people working in various fields enables students to experience an environment that they have heard about but never encountered firsthand.

Practical Tips for Creating a College-Going Culture in Schools

Although creating a fully effective college-going culture requires a concerted, system-wide effort by administrators, teachers, and counselors alike, there are a variety of straightforward projects that schools and/ or individual faculty can institute to begin seeding such an environment. If the key components discussed earlier lay out a strategy for building the college-going culture, these practical illustrations begin to chart out some of the tactics one might employ. Over the years, my colleagues and I have encountered dozens of novel and innovative ways to promote college readiness in students. The next sections describe but a few of them.

Reenvision Group Work

Reenvisioning group work involves the creation of intentional groups, rather than having students self-select their teams. This might mean creating a diversity of experiences in a group, or deliberately creating teams that force more advanced students to interact—perhaps even rely on—students who might not typically excel or engage. Students learn from being able to teach, so how do you create intentional groups in which students might learn from one another? An assignment that requires both the scholarly attention of some high-achieving students and the personal experience and cultural relevance of a struggling student encourages participation and input from both participants.

Utilize Good-Faith Assignments

Good-faith assignments, such as the example noted earlier, can undergird a student's self-efficacy and academic self-concept by assessing work, at least in part, on metrics that each student can readily achieve. So rather than grading a student on syntax and grammar, a good-faith assignment might seek to tap into the knowledge he or she brings to the group or the classroom. If it is an assignment that allows students to talk about something they know about—their home, their community, or their environment—they can confidently share their expertise and earn a good grade. These assignments do not replace the core educational requirements, but they help build students' academic self-concept in ways that, eventually, give them the wherewithal to tackle those challenges too.

Become an Interior Decorator and a Proud Alum

Colleges and universities have no better champions than their alumni. Teachers can demonstrate their school pride in the classroom, building a college-tinged environment while also serving as an ambassador of higher education in general. We all, especially as children, absorb elements of our surroundings. And hey, who doesn't enjoy the occasional chance to talk up their alma mater? Each classroom representing one specific school enables students at the middle school and high school levels specifically to learn about many different colleges and universities as they go from period to period, increasing their exposure to an array of college and universities.

Monthly College Days and College Rallies (Students and Teachers)

Taking the proud-alum concept one step further, teachers, teacher groups, or school-wide faculty and administration might create college days, when everyone celebrates a university or set of universities. Perhaps everyone wears a college T-shirt or sweatshirt. A district might even get local colleges to donate paraphernalia to support the rallies, leaving students with gear that, who knows, might help sway their higher-education decisions in the future. One college counselor in South Los Angeles established "College-Gear Day" at her middle school. This was a uniformed school, but students got to wear college gear one day a month, which was a welcome change from their daily monotonous attire. These monthly college days do not have to involve full-fledged fairs or an entire event that takes a lot of planning and effort from school staff, but can merely include a lunchtime rally or simply wearing college paraphernalia. A huge annual college fair is great and gives students insight into the wide variety of options they might have after high school, but monthly college days provide the sorts of consistent exposure that help establish a persistent college-going culture.

Power in Naming

Some schools have shifted the terms they use, both in classrooms but even for students themselves, and I have observed a remarkable effectiveness in some of these changes. Some schools, for example, refer to young people as scholars rather than students, and teachers work to evoke the cognitive and creative extension that the term implies. This sort of renaming elicits a sort of distinction that students can see themselves. Other schools have shifted the structure of block schedules to more closely resemble university courses, or they have renamed schedule blocks to reflect different colleges or universities. Even simply naming things differently can influence students' perspectives and create a stronger college-going culture.

Have the Conversation

Students often perceive their teachers as superheroes or as alien entities. They are surprised when they see teachers at the grocery store or find out they have kids of their own: "You have a life outside these doors?!?" Students many times have difficulty accepting that their teachers weren't born teachers and have little knowledge of their teachers' educational journey. Sometimes, it is as simple as having a conversation about what it took for you to get to where you are that humanizes and actualizes. There is power in telling students you didn't get straight As your entire life, or that you struggled at times in college and even changed your major a couple of times. A teacher's background story not only humanizes the teacher but also, more important, provides a reference point for the student that he or she did not have before. Some teachers make sharing their life a game; others add it in as a weekly event, a story about their experience and about their road to college. Ultimately, these conversations reveal that everyone has peaks and valleys, and hearing about teachers' road to and through higher education is critical for students to hear.

Exposure

As noted earlier, exposure is a huge part of creating a college- and career-going culture, but it does not have to be a grand program or field trip to Big State University. Teachers have come up with a variety of ways to bring the college experience into the classroom and expose students to various careers. One might split the class into teams on both sides of a divisive topic and then ask a couple of local attorneys to describe the idea of a law school's moot court and prep the teams for debate. Or more simply, one might bring in a college friend who has come to visit and have her talk about her career and how she got there. Bring her to the classroom to share, or have a school-wide assembly with a handful of local owners of small businesses. Exposure does not always have to be a field trip away from the school; it can involve bringing surrounding community members and personal networks into the school.

Leverage Community Partnerships to Present Multiple Pathways

Sometimes we don't readily think to offer this career exposure. We might do a better job of providing exposure to colleges and universities than we do to different career and vocational pathways. We can remedy that by bringing in folks to talk to our students: a beautician who talks about beauty school and licensing requirements for the job, a mechanic who started out as an apprentice at a dealership and then made the leap to open his own garage. These visits expose students to other career trajectories that they might never have thought about otherwise—and provide that wide variety of options in hopes of finding a career that resonates with every student in the room and taps into students' natural talents that they might not even know could be part of a viable career option.

Know Your Role, Biases, and Limits

Teachers are care providers, not just educators. Each one has a critical role in caring for students. Collectively, we need to do more to help teachers embrace their role as caregivers and figure out how they can best serve students. As noted earlier, providing care does not mean addressing all the challenges and ills a child suffers. In fact, small, everyday affirmations and supportive words often have a more powerful effect on a student's self-efficacy and self-image. Taking time as an administrator to know your students' names and asking about their day can humanize you in students' eyes—*and them in your eyes, too.* Do you know why that student is always in trouble or always late? Simply taking the time to hear students is an important part of creating and demonstrating a culture of care.

Teachers, counselors, and administrators also need to take stock of their biases. Which students do we think are destined for greatness, and which students do we not engage with as much? How we categorize students and stratify them into different groups and classifications—even in our own minds—affects how we treat them. Teachers might never verbalize their biases, but young people know when teachers already have a way of seeing them, and they can read both the implicit and explicit biases teachers have toward certain sets of students.

In discussing the role of being an educator and care provider, educators do not often talk about their personal limitations. Teachers note with pride how well their students do despite the school's limited resources, but they far less often discuss the toll that supporting such achievement takes on their own lives. In addition to all the creativity, passion, and expertise a teacher brings to the classroom, does he or she also bring the stress and the raggedness that comes with providing those personal energies? Self-care, for both students and teachers, is a critical element of an effective college-going culture, and we need to talk more about the day-to-day limitations we all face.

KEY TAKEAWAYS

- A college-going culture provides a broader array of postsecondary options for students and is especially vital in improving the college enrollment and completion rates for students of color. Although creating the most effective college-going culture requires a comprehensive effort across a school district or system, teachers can use a variety of easily digestible and implementable projects to make school more relevant for students—and make students more resilient for the challenges they will face along the way.

- School communities in general and educators in particular need to recognize the impact that social and cultural supports have on both students' academic success and our belief in their potential. Making this significant shift in mindset—recognizing teachers' indispensable role in the care for and belief in students—can make a huge difference in academic achievement and preparation for higher education.

- To make these sorts of shifts and create a true college-going culture, schools and communities must provide teachers with the support they need. The responsibility of care for and belief in students must extend beyond the classroom, especially when financial and similar resources are limited.

Questions from the Field

In our conversations with teachers, very important questions regarding creating a college-going culture arise. The following are a few that I hope are helpful in your work with students.

> 1. *How much of creating a college-going culture falls on teachers, and how much on guidance counselors or college counselors? Given that teachers' capacity is stretched so thin as it is, what more can they do?*

Creating a college-going culture is a school-wide effort. It is not only a teacher's responsibility, or only a counselor's, or the sole responsibility of the family. Some might suggest that it is all up to parents to provide that environment and capacity for students, but everyone plays a role. That is why in this work, we often talk about the small things teachers can do. If you can make that one small shift, it might impact one student. It isn't difficult to provide richer feedback to our students or to be more affirming or to create group assignments that allow our students to engage with one another. If we can think about this in terms of smaller shifts and not overall changes or overhauls, we have options that we can accommodate.

There is a role for counselors, of course. Maybe part of that is to go to the workshops conducted by the different colleges and universities, so that the counselors learn each year about updates in admissions requirements. The University of California system has a UC Counselor's Conference every year. Counselors can also be readers for college applications at different colleges and universities, which provides a different level of insight that they can use to advise students. So rather than getting too caught up in the huge transformational pieces, I try to get people to think about the things they can do at a small scale that may help the counselor, help the school, or help the teacher make a shift that is not too overwhelming.

2. *How can teachers, administrators, and counselors stay up to date with the constantly shifting and increasingly competitive college entrance requirements?*

Many admissions officers and college and university recruiters are charged with going out to different schools, and particularly to different communities and neighborhoods—both those that have historically sent students to their school and those that have not. Sometimes just bringing those individuals to the campus again and getting them in front of more faculty and staff is helpful. So when we bring college representatives to campus to see students, we can also make sure that counselors and administrators learn more from the college representatives as well. Sometimes keeping up to date also involves going to the conferences, workshops, and seminars that many of these schools offer. We might not always have the time to attend or even know that these events are happening, so tasking a couple of counselors with keeping an ear to the ground for new updates will help all of us advise students better. Even then, we need also to consider the different colleges or universities in which students might have interest, but with which we have no relationship. Even beyond getting the school to send information, providing opportunities for teachers and counselors to learn more about colleges of interest to students is important.

How do we forge relationships with these schools and build a sense of connection? That might involve appointing a liaison between the university and the school, someone who sits in a college center and regularly meets with students who express interest in that school and/or its programs. The connections established with university representatives can provide resources to help us understand what is happening on their campus, and then how we can integrate that into the college-going culture on our own campus. Those conversations are useful as well.

3. *College isn't for everyone, so why do we even talk about this? Why do we talk about "college ready for all" if all students aren't going to college?*

    We have to expand the way we think about "college ready" to accommodate the notion that we want all students to have that option if they so choose. It is really about providing all students with the opportunity and the resources for them to make that decision. We have to create an environment in which students are equipped to be able to make that decision come senior year because we provided them with the information and resources along the way. I think we also need to consider expanding the terminology to "college and career going" instead of simply "college going." Part of that is exposing students to other trade, vocational, and career opportunities that they might not come into contact with otherwise. That could include apprenticeships and shadowing opportunities to provide a pathway and exposure opportunities to vocational and trade arenas. That consistent exposure, again, puts students in a better position come senior year to make a decision, because they have seen and learned about a variety of options and opportunities.

Recommended Resources

Conley, D. (2007). *Redefining college readiness.* Eugene, OR: Educational Policy Improvement Center. Conley provides a comprehensive definition of college readiness, and strategies for developing and achieving essential skill sets. Segments of this reading also focus on providing relevant information for schools and students to foster college readiness.

Knight, M. G., & Marciano, J. E. (2013). *College ready: Preparing black and Latina/o youth for higher education—A culturally relevant approach.* New York, NY: Teachers College Press. This book highlights the narratives and perspectives of Black and Latinx students and families and includes the supports and hindrances related to their college readiness and access. This book provides support for teachers and school administrators in creating a culturally relevant, school-wide, college-going culture.

Conley, D. (2010). *College and career ready: Helping all students succeed beyond high school.* San Francisco, CA: Jossey-Bass. This book describes best practices and clear examples of what actual high schools are doing to foster college and career readiness. The uniqueness of this book is its intentional inclusion of career readiness and work preparedness for all students.

Curry, J. R. (2015). African Americans and career and college readiness. In J. R. Curry & M. A. Shillingford (Eds.), *African American students' career and college readiness: The journey unraveled.* Lanham,

MD: Lexington Books. This chapter provides a historical and contemporary look at the educational attainment of African American students in a quest for college and career readiness. With the inclusion of a social and political lens, this resource identifies barriers, new innovations, and implementable approaches to creating a college- and career-going culture for Black students.

Howard, T. C., Tunstall, J. D., & Flennaugh, T. K. (Eds.) (2016). *Expanding college access for urban youth: What schools and colleges can do.* **New York, NY: Teachers College Press.** This book highlights a social justice–oriented school–university partnership that successfully provides students of color access to some of the most selective and prestigious universities across the nation. Featuring firsthand accounts from student participants, the book documents the program model that comprises the support, mentoring, curriculum, and resources needed to transform the college opportunities for underrepresented youth from underserved communities.

7

"It's Not So Much . . . for a Grade"

Humanization as Real Social and Emotional Learning

PATRICK CAMANGIAN

On September 13, 2018, Shawn Ginwright, one of the first education scholars linking educational equity and research in the health sciences, tweeted, "Despite its popularity, social and emotional learning (SEL) may be particularly harmful to kids of color." Six hours later, Pedro Noguera, a Distinguished Professor at UCLA, well known for his international work on educational transformation, replied, "Exercise can be harmful, too if you do it wrong. The same applies to SEL. To ignore it is a bigger problem."

Although Ginwright's critique of SEL is an indictment of some of the irrelevant ways it has been taken up by schools and districts across the country, Noguera's response is a commentary on the role of communities of color in making education responsive to the needs of its children. On one hand, a color-blind approach to SEL too often views students of color through a deficit-thinking model that "contends that minority cultural values . . . are dysfunctional, and therefore cause low educational and occupational attainment."[1] On the other hand, if educators do not make SEL critically relevant, then the holistic needs of students of color will remain unaddressed.

What exactly is social and emotional learning? According to professors Joseph Zins and Maurice Elias, SEL "is the capacity to recognize and manage emotions, solve problems effectively, and establish positive relationships with others."[2] Further, Elias summarizes SEL research as being based on one fundamental principle: "Effective, lasting academic learning and SEL are built on caring relationships and warm but challenging classroom and school environments."[3] Teachers must understand how students' social and emotional health is shaped by their experiences with the structural violence—a form of violence that involves a social structure or institution—of ghetto schooling, economic underdevelopment, and rape culture, to name a few.[4] They must engage students in ways that help them more effectively manage fear, anxiety, grief, powerlessness, and other various forms of social toxicity that come as a result of structural violence.[5]

To address what it means to make SEL critically relevant for students of color, teachers must aim for **humanization**. How teachers take up and approach SEL still falls far short of transforming the dehumanizing structures that impose self-hate, divide-and-conquer tactics, and suboppression, and consequently harm the social and emotional health and well-being of young people of color. Humanization requires that students learn the following three concepts:

- Knowledge of self
- Solidarity
- Self-determination

Humanization provides the real social and emotional learning that historically marginalized communities deserve. By lacking an explicit analysis of the intersecting systems of racism, sexism, homophobia, and classism, SEL is not encompassing enough of a framework to address the dehumanization that marginalized communities experience. Fulfilling the aims of SEL does not ensure humanization, whereas fulfilling the objectives of humanization does ensure that teachers are addressing the social and emotional needs of marginalized students. SEL and humanization need to work together.

The problem is, color-blind approaches to SEL compound the harm done by intersecting systems of oppression by placing the burden of responsibility for change on the people who are harmed the most—students of color, gender-nonconforming youth, and young people whose families bear the brunt of economic disparities in underdeveloped communities. It's important that those with privilege do not take ahistorical and color-blind approaches to co-opting notions of humanization, arguing that all people have similar human conditions and that thus teachers should treat everyone the same. The reality is that all people do not have similar conditions or experiences. Therefore, I'm talking about self-care, building a sense of community, and defining success in relation to one's community—imperatives into which those with privilege too often do not have much insight. This is not a hokey, hopeful misinterpretation of humanization that fails to look at historical oppression, hegemony, or dehumanization.[6] In this chapter, I'll accomplish the following three goals: describe the importance of humanization in the form of knowledge of self, solidarity, and self-determination; illustrate what these tenets look like in practice; and conclude with relevant resources, as well as questions for deeper reflection.

From Self-Hate to Knowledge of Self

To move students from self-hate to a knowledge of self, educators need to transition them from being objects of racially hostile, community-irrelevant curriculum to being the actual subject of their own studies. When individuals are objects of history, their sense of self is shaped by the social and status quo forces in their life. This often leads to self-hate, a strong dislike of oneself, especially on the basis of cultural, gendered, and economic identities. When students are not the subjects of their own learning and studies, they do not understand the world from their point of view, they fear what they do not understand, and they hate what they fear—themselves.

They, then, become their own worst enemies.

Although people can choose their responses to the values of dominant society, their sense of self is often shaped by the social systems and values of the culture of western civilization. Thus the perspective distributed and deposited into the collective consciousness of people and students of color usually weakens their racial, gendered, and class-based sense of self. Through racist, sexist, classist, and homophobic school curricula, young people are required to navigate a course of study that rarely positions them as the actual subjects of their own studies. This means that who students are, what they experience, and how they have been shaped individually, collectively, and culturally are rarely the focus of what they study in schools. School curricula exclude the knowledge, stories, histories, struggles, and experiences of people of color and other marginalized populations, including but certainly not limited to women, the poor, and LGBTQ individuals and communities.

In essence, students of color learn about themselves, their communities, and their culture based on the experiences and perspectives of others—too often from perspectives that are at odds with the history and dignity of their people.

Developing a knowledge of self is often a struggle because students of color rarely have the opportunity to describe the world from their perspective. With this being the case, educators should "flip the script." This means educators "must equip students with the analytic tools to unpack dominant and non-dominant discourses and histories."[7] This holds true not just with content knowledge but with social and emotional learning as well. To develop knowledge of self, communities and students of color have to be involved in examining, explaining, and interpreting the world no longer as objects but as the subjects of their own humanity. Similarly, Paulo Freire, a leading advocate of critical pedagogy, asserted, "To exist, humanly, is to name the world, to change it."[8] To do so, students must study their humanity with compassion, love, and understanding. Given the Eurocentric, male-dominant, and heteronormative context of miseducation that has shaped much of people of color's sense of self, this may require "both teachers and students to painfully examine [their] lives and actions within an unjust society and to share the sensibility that pain may pave the path to justice."[9]

And this raises a key concept: a significant part of the social and emotional learning that students of color must engage in should allow them to grieve, celebrate, and root for themselves in a society that does otherwise.

From Divide and Conquer to Solidarity

To help students move from being divided and conquered to having solidarity and a knowledge of self, teachers have to end what psychiatrist and philosopher Franz Fanon described as horizontal violence.[10] Horizontal violence occurs when historically oppressed people participate in the oppression of one another. In general, when people of color hate themselves, they usually distrust people who look just like them and experience life as they do. In essence, they tend to project their self-hate onto people who remind them of their own suffering. In this sense, people of color are taught, for all intents and purposes, to hate people who may recognize in them what they recognize in one another, when they project their own false sense of inferiority onto people with whom they should most identify.

All of this shows up in how students of color perform in their classes, interact with one another in schools, fight with one another, insult their peers, and care less about curriculum they cannot relate to. Further, the conflicts that occur in communities of color migrate into schools and present themselves to teachers in their classrooms. Fanon suggested educating students of color to heed Malcolm X's call to recognize people of color's common history, which could help define our common purpose.[11] Authentic solidarity is grounded in a "continued commitment to [a] group . . . [where] one begins to understand the connections of struggles."[12]

To build solidarity as a response to the phenomenon of miseducation, teachers should develop their students' ideological clarity, build a sense of community based on this clarity, and hold each other accountable to a common purpose. According to University of Massachusetts professor Lilia Bartolome, ideological clarity "refers to the process by which individuals achieve a deepening awareness of the sociopolitical and economic realities that shape their lives and capacity to recreate them."[13] In other words, teachers must facilitate learning that helps students understand how history is present in the moment. This process includes examining who has power in society, by asking two questions:

- How did those segments of society acquire power?
- Who are the people in positions of powerlessness?

Ultimately, ideological clarity demands that educators analyze these inequities of power in the interest of marginalized people.

For students of color to understand the prevailing social forces to struggle against, such as wealth inequality, patriarchy, and racial inequity, they may transform the fragmentation imposed on them by channeling that personal frustration and social dissatisfaction against the social systems that undermine their collective communities. These social systems include, but are not limited to, disinvestment in communities of color, mass incarceration, anti-immigrant and anti-Muslim public policy, and heteronormativity. Teachers, then, must have a clear understanding of the evolution of the existing social order and figure out how students can heal their fractured relationships with each other and transform their relationship to their common oppression.

To understand their experiences with a common oppression, at the most basic level, students of color need space to first work to communicate through their perceived differences and build community together long before we try to advance any type of political rationale. As they sort out these tensions among themselves, they start to define their common purpose. It's the teacher's role to design learning activities that help students share their experiences with various systems of oppression, which oftentimes intersect across two or more forms—racism and White supremacy, sexism and misogyny, classism, homophobia, and more.

After students' share their experiences with one another, teachers should help students explore the collective needs of their communities based on the struggles that students identified. Knowledge of self requires students to explore existential questions such as "Who am I?" and "What experiences have I had that have shaped my identity?" and "How do I see the world?" We can help students find a common purpose by asking such questions as "What do your individual and collective perspectives and responses to the immediate social conditions of your lives mean for your community?" and "Based on your common, and diverging, experiences, what does your community need, and what does this mean for us, individually and collectively?"

By understanding the big picture, students can recognize that what they believe they don't like about one another's personalities is actually a symptom of the social trauma they experience on the margins of society. They learn that their own experience is not an isolated one, but rather one that other marginalized people go through. For example, the xenophobia that undocumented people experience may look and feel a lot different than the rape culture that female-bodied folks are too often vulnerable to. Similarly, the anti-Black racism of police brutality in African American communities is different than the homophobic violence that LGBTQ people are exposed to. When viewing one another through the lenses disseminated through dominant narratives, it is easy to project cultural biases onto people who are affected by these perspectives. When young people are allowed to share how their points of view are shaped by their lived experiences, however, they begin to see that they have much more in common with one another. Upon understanding this commonality, students are much more open to studying the systems of oppression that have shaped their experiences—and, we hope, use what they learn in order to transform those systems.

The importance of this togetherness cannot be overstated; this solidarity serves as the basis of students' community purpose and kinship.

From Suboppression to Self-Determination

Suboppression comes when oppressed people define their success in terms of the image and interests of their oppressors.[14] To move from suboppression to self-determination, students of color have to transition from hegemonic consent—meaning that they may be complicit in their own oppression—to practicing dissent and disrupting dehumanization as it surfaces in their everyday lives.

Without knowledge of self, and without solidarity, students of color rarely have the critical consciousness to make decisions in their own interests, or in the interests of the people they love; for the communities where they exist; or for their cultures. Too often, students do exactly as intersecting systems of oppression want them to do. Unknowingly, they become suboppressors whose humanity is based on their desire to achieve the freedoms assumed by those in more privileged positions. When young people of color adopt the worldview of their oppressor, they are always experiencing the psychological violence of a secondhand philosophy that governs their conformity, reactionary behavior, or self-defeating resistance.[15] In these cases, cultural assimilation or academic disinvestment is internalized, rationalized, and reproduced as the only viable form of agency to act against a degrading educational culture.

In this way, self-determination is less about succumbing to status quo norms. Instead, it's about constructing notions of self in service and relation to oppressed people regardless of whatever notions of humanity have been narrowly defined by systems of power. In this sense, self-determination is purpose-driven, practical application, "the authentic union of action and reflection."[16] Rather than defining success only in terms of their own individual pursuits, students of color must understand and coconstruct notions of success that also help advance the collective needs of the communities they are a part of—otherwise, their personal pursuits may advance them toward upward mobility at the expense of their communities.

The key for both educators and students lies in understanding that success for marginalized people means something different than success for those with privilege.

When teachers believe that the most promising pathway for their students is to distance themselves from the communities with which they most identify, they are—knowingly or not—teaching those students to conform to systems of oppression. This runs counter to the purpose of education from the perspective of self-determination, which is to study in order to transform the social oppression responsible for a community's misery.

Teaching for self-determination takes into account the following questions:

- What is their purpose as students and people of color?
- How does their purpose align with the needs of historically marginalized people?
- How does this purpose guide their decision-making?
- What does all of this mean for the larger social groups they are a part of?

When students reflect on their responsibilities to themselves, their communities, and the world, they often realize that they were rarely taught to be clear about the purpose of their academic identities. How they spend time thinking about their lives as young people of color determines how they spend their time as students.

For many teachers, engaging students of color and other marginalized students with questions like these is a new experience. These educators must reflect on the ways in which schooling has benefited them and served their needs, as well as how they've had more success navigating the system compared to the young people they teach. This requires that they be self-critical and that they question a world that benefits those who have the most. To do so, they should try their hardest to understand, on their students' terms, the experiences and circumstances of those who have the least. For teachers to engage their students in this way, they must learn to be comfortable in their discomfort and to trust their students' ability to teach them when they articulate their experiences with social oppression—especially when the teachers feel implicated in students' indictments against those systems.

Admittedly, this is very difficult.

It's acceptable, and understandable, if one has never considered these types of questions. It's not necessary to have answers to these questions, either. In fact, if teachers are honest with their students about not having ever considered questions like these, they would enable their students to trust them more because of the shared interpersonal and intercultural vulnerabilities. Because schools are more often places that pose surface-level inquiries, students may not be prepared to engage in this type of introspection. When teachers commit to connecting their teaching to their students' experiences, however, they will slowly but surely be more effective at teaching their students to determine their own needs and the destinies they desire for themselves and the people whom they care about.

If students of color lack the proper purpose, they'll lack the proper perspective to examine academic and social and emotional health and well-being. Being self-determining students requires that they acquire academic literacies that are critical, transformative, and humanizing. It is not an either-or approach; it is a both-and approach. It is both academically rigorous and humanizing, meaning that teachers must look for changes in achievement patterns beyond the classroom, because traditional notions of academic success are too limited. Sure, students must not just meet but exceed the standards of academic success. But beyond that, they need the type of learning that leads to holistic growth and social transformation in their communities.

Social and Emotional Learning in Practice

I put my ideas related to SEL into practice in an Expository Composition course during the second unit of the school year,[17] taking place at a high school that had the city's largest Black student population (66.1 percent) for a large, comprehensive campus. Most of the students lived in the surrounding working-class, working-poor, and surviving-poor community. The cultural makeup was unique in relation to the rest of the city, as its 72.4 percent Black population made it one of the few remaining predominantly Black communities—with an influx of Latinx residents.

The key skills required by the state learning standards for Expository Composition were for students to be able to identify, distinguish, analyze, critique, respond, prepare, interpret, articulate, and compare. Key concepts included understanding genres; persuasion; expository, narrative, persuasive, research, and compare-and-contrast essays; vocabulary; grammar/mechanics; oral communication; and historical concepts. As someone who aims to have critically relevant interpretations of state learning standards, I always find it important to ask, "What's missing?" As far as some skills and content are concerned, I also wanted to teach students to critique canonical texts, media, and theory; utilize theory, sanctioned academic English, socially relevant and politically empowering texts, and their community cultural wealth; and be able to challenge, question, embody, and apply what they are studying.

My focus fulfilled an acknowledged SEL aim to teach students to "recognize and manage emotions," "solve problems effectively," and "establish positive relationships with others,"[18] while honoring research which found that "the best course for many youths is to remain securely anchored in their ethnic communities while they pursue a strategy of selective acculturation or segmented assimilation."[19] The following three objectives guided the critical approach to the course:

- Identify some of the most pressing issues facing students in their communities
- Expose students to theories of self and social transformation
- Synthesize key ideas for student essays, presentations, and application to their everyday lives

The following example took place at the beginning of the school year. Students were sharing the preliminary stages of their writing, revealing the ways they constructed their varying cultural identities. I prompted student narratives with the following questions:

- What do you stand for?
- What experiences have you had that made you this way?
- Who do you want to become?
- How are you going to become this way?
- What does this mean for your community?

Guiding questions like these position students to engage in the type of critical self-reflection too often absent in their schooling, pushing them to spend time interrogating their own identities, in the hope that doing so would increase students' knowledge of themselves. Asking students to critically reflect on their identities triggered a dialogue that included students' beginning to hold each other accountable to the perceived needs of their community. The following dialogue illustrates the ways in which youth firmly challenged one another to understand the consequences of their reactionary behavior, examine notions of power along racial lines, and call for fundamental social change. For example, Tyjuan responded to Leon's proud proclamations of being gang affiliated, violently enforcing his identity on others:

> We're divided. When you go to a White community, they're one . . . Over here, we're . . . holding the next person down. Our priorities aren't up to standard. In White communities, they focus on power. On money. On helping one another prosper. But as far as us, we're trying to hold the other person down.

Tyjuan's commentary pointed to the divide-and-conquer mentality he had witnessed in his community, implying instead a need for the type of solidarity that would advance the social position of the people he most identifies with. Tyjuan's perspective on the existence of White solidarity, however accurate or inaccurate it might be, showed how he had experienced power being highly concentrated in European American communities in contrast to his own.

As a rebuttal, Leon offered his viewpoint on the phenomenon: "That's the funny thing cuz that's all [we] know how to do. It's hard to . . . get a job . . . But it's real easy to . . . hit a lick [do something illegal to make money]."

Leon, in essence, argued that being divided and conquered as a community comes as a result of being alienated from employment and resources more readily accessible to outside (most likely White) communities.

Reflecting on his point, Tyjuan replied, "Feel you. I mean, they already feel like they at their lowest point."

The exchange marked an understanding of the economic struggle facing many in their community. On one hand, Tyjuan argued that the systemic divide-and-conquer approach is holding down Black people. On the other hand, he replied to Leon that he understood where they were coming from in their economically underdeveloped community. Together, they validated each other's perspectives as young Black men struggling through the material conditions of their lives. This was a show of solidarity. This solidarity was forged as a result of students' sharing their knowledge of self. Beginning the academic year in this way was intentional—with the intention being for students to identify some of their most pressing issues. The guiding questions of the unit aimed to help students study self-hate and the divide-and-conquer framework in their everyday lives. Knowledge of self and gestures of solidarity came as a result of a classroom space that enabled students to discuss their experiences on their own terms.

This dialogue became a springboard for critical discussion. Stephen told Leon, "That's what they want you to do. That's what they want you to think."

Janelle added, "They want you to give up. When people think like you, you holding us down."

Rather than trying to silence oppositional perspectives, dialoguing about their common experiences helped students come to a collective conclusion about being divided as a community and thus more easily conquered as a people. Leon seemed to open up to the class's critique of his lifestyle by raising his brows, nodding up and down, and pondering their thoughts. In that moment, he was gaining knowledge of self. He was learning about the effects of divide-and-conquer policies, and he was processing the relevance of having solidarity. Yet, as students kept identifying the tensions within their community, Leon became defensive and declared, "Nobody can convince me that I'm wrong. Nobody in this world can convince me that what I've done or what I'm doing is wrong. Anything I ever did."

Although they were able to discuss the tension of behaving in ways that reinforce the oppression facing Black people, Leon was not willing to admit that the use of force or his criminal undertakings were wrong. The reflection in which he was engaging is common for students when discussing the conflicting aspects of their social identities and the tensions between self-hate and knowledge of self. The collision of prior ideas occupying the same space with other possibilities plays out in students' thought processes because that collision signifies the cognitive dissonance of resisting conclusions that seem obvious, but this collision of thoughts is often part of humanizing learning.

The intensity in the room was palpable; as students spoke with—and often, over—each other, more of them began raising their hands to offer their perspectives on Leon's stance. Each opinion offered was an opportunity for students to develop knowledge of self, as the positions they took strengthened the ways they understood particular circumstances that their community faces and their individual relationships to it. One student argued that gang mentalities similar to Leon's acted on a person's fear of competing against the rest of society for a more widely legitimate approach to improving her or his quality of life. A young woman asked why he was willing to weaken the Black community; another pled for Leon to plan for his own future and change his ways.

The attention drove Leon to argue defensively: "Don't nobody think three years down the line . . . cuz you could die any moment in South Central, man. Any given day." Here, Leon expressed that long-term planning was not his priority because his lived experience did not offer enough evidence for him to believe in his own chances of survival. Due to his acute awareness of his surroundings, Leon was fatalistically worried about death, which loomed for him and for many people in his community. Interrogating this collectively helped Leon engage in public knowledge of self as he was becoming clearer about the social context of his individual decision-making. Students continued to engage in a discussion that focused on Leon's pressing concerns.

Rather than limit their classroom experience to the ahistorical and impersonal ways that schooling has been shaped by official curricula, this prompting, to which students responded among a classroom community, opened up the space for youth to reflect on essential issues of immediate relevance to their community. Central to the development of solidarity among teachers and students in urban contexts is the willingness to engage in "real talk," or open and honest conversations that address the questions with which the young people are most concerned. Later, during an interview, Leon said of this process, "I think you was like, [messing] with our ideas. You [messed] with mine, I could tell you" (*laughs*).

I asked him how these processes affected his learning.

Leon answered, "I wanna say . . . at first . . . it didn't make me want to change myself; it made me want to question myself. And then as the class went along, it made me really want to change some of the things I did."

Such authentic dialogue, however, necessitates that teachers create the spaces for students to connect and develop deeper understandings of each other, so that all forms of dialogue work to improve the overall quality of the classroom culture. Beyond cultivating "safe" spaces for dialogue, we must foster classroom cultures that critically nurture the ability for both teachers and students to confront the painful parts of our lives and the struggles facing oppressed people.[20]

The student work I focus on in the next paragraphs comes from a unit in which students read socially provocative texts to construct philosophies for social change. In the first example, Leon analyzes "The Willie Lynch Letter." In a fictional speech supposedly delivered on the bank of the James River in Virginia in 1712, William Lynch claimed to have a "foolproof method" for controlling Africans in the United States for "at least 300 years," which then led to a program of atrocious mental conditioning. Covering the "Warning: Possible Interloping Negatives" section of "The Willie Lynch Letter," Leon spoke about Black history being stolen, and expressed his anger toward the ways that people of color's reality was defined by White supremacist thought. He answered the questions, "Do these psychological effects still exist? Where and how?"

Having students apply their interpretations of socially relevant texts to their current social context is a pedagogical attempt for them to identify the ways that many of the problems in their lives are part of a history of oppression that preceded their experiences with it. Sharing their analysis with one another helps students understand that what they experience as individuals is often a result of experiencing a similar system of oppression. This helps students find a commonality—and build community—across perceived differences. Examining his world with the words from the text, Leon spoke scathingly about his understanding of reality:

> I feel like [these psychological effects still exist], for the simple fact . . . the idea of the image of a beautiful African changed. Like, you see a beautiful woman or something, you think light skin, long hair . . . And when you think of an ugly [Black person] . . . you think, dark skinned . . . nappy hair. When you think dark skin, you think dirty. It's not that it makes you less of a person for thinking that, it's just the [lies] that [were] embedded in your brain, like your whole mental thought process.

In addition to pointing out the consequences of internalized oppression, Leon combined his reading ability with his critical analysis and his cultural voice, leading him to communicate with an empowered oral intensity. Text and context coalesced as he connected to his audience and the classroom discourse. Leon provided a critically relevant interpretation of "The Willie Lynch Letter" that reflected the students' immediate community realities.

When considering that the desires of the oppressed are often guided by their appreciation of their oppressors' humanity—in this case, standards of physical attractiveness—Leon offered an honest evaluation of the ways he saw this normalized in his community:

> As far as cross breeding, it still goes on, but it's not forced upon each other. It's like . . . tradition . . . the [thing] to do. In order to make a pretty baby, and the idea of a pretty baby is like, "I want it to be light skinned, and it's gonna have curly hair." . . . And you go off and meet you a nice lil' partner, that's light-skinned with curly hair, green eyes, [etc.]. And the baby comes out looking less and less Black and losing what they were in the first place. . . We losing sight of what our people originally were. So due to that, we lose sight of what a true beautiful African is, due to our own crossbreeding.

Leon, arguably, essentializes Blackness and Black beauty through the promotion of monoraciality, which we must help students complicate. In terms of the early development of his consciousness, however, his critique of oppressive discourse defining beauty in their community was aimed at the ways Africans—like many people of color worldwide—aspire to alter perceived levels of physical attractiveness based on their internalized oppression. In this way, Leon illuminated his observations regarding how Black communities sometimes aspire toward notions of attractiveness that are based on paradigms that socially devalue the phenotypical traits of people of color worldwide, and especially African-type features. Despite "the unwillingness by African Americans to discuss or perhaps even admit to their personal struggles associated with attractiveness,"[21] Leon critically engaged often deeply sensitive, yet unnamed, intraracial tensions of the community in which a majority of the students were members.

Upon completion of his presentation, Leon simultaneously expressed his frustration as a man of color, called attention to his growing anger, and also moved toward developing a strategy of social transformation. Leon talked in relation to his own plan of action, answering the "How do you feel about this and why?" question for his group's assigned reading:

> I felt kind of stupid, not just for myself, but for all people of color. Because it is a cycle, and their plan worked. It worked hella good. And

> I realized that [it] is still working. So in my eyes, they like re-created the image of like [a beautiful Black person] and I thought about it, and they could create the image of anything. And it gets to the point where they keep remaking and remaking everything, and you start seeing the world through the same glasses they looking at. But, you not realizing it because you have no true history. You only have . . . what they left you with, what they told you is true. . . I'm kind of upset, and lost at the same time.

Revealing his sense of humiliation, Leon connected this emotion with his frustration over a dominant White culture's ability to obscure reality among people of color. His disappointment was pointed at the vulnerability of people of color when they were missing a clear sense of their own histories. Leon's anger, coupled with confusion, was a result of the grim reality that a system of oppression actually worked and that its objects of domination were defenseless against the ideologies imposed on them.

This is an example of knowledge of self, solidarity, and self-determination. Leon's presentation illustrates knowledge of self as he showed awareness of his community reality, vulnerability, and needs. By identifying a common oppression among Black people and describing the importance of uniting as a community, Leon is arguing for solidarity. By expressing the need for Black people to have independent thought, he is declaring self-determination as a necessary pathway for his people moving forward.

Socially relevant, provocative assignments help arouse students' critical curiosities, stimulate academic engagement, and apply critical perspectives concerning their histories as people of color. Leon was able to make connections between two women of color's experiences as marginalized people and connect it to his struggle as a young Black man:

> Anzaldua's [*Borderlands/La Frontera*] . . . how she was talking about she had three choices: to be a nun, a housewife, or a hooker . . . then I apply it to what I'm doing as a young Black man in an urban community, I only have three choices: I'ma pick up a gun, or a basketball, or rap, or I'ma sell dope. It's like damn, that really connects . . . and it make you wonder why. . . When I read Audre Lorde, I seen that . . . our own people, like she was getting hated on by other Black men as a lesbian. And that's the same [thing] that White people do to us.

Engaging readings that help students demystify their oppression are important for them to understand concrete, historical ways to explain their current condition as oppressed people. This form of critical analysis is essential for them to "recognize and manage [their] emotions."

Beyond being a pedagogical intervention used to motivate students, "solv[ing] problems effectively" and "establish[ing] positive relationships with others" in critically relevant ways are also skill sets that SEL must foster in order to disrupt systemic and interpersonal dehumanization as it exists in students' immediate realities. The accumulation of these types of assessments prepare them to "recognize and manage [their] emotions," "solve problems effectively," and "establish positive relationships with others" outside their classes as well. As an important tenet of critically relevant SEL, self-determination provides students assessments that enable them to achieve the second and third goals despite learning standards and frameworks that lack this imperative.

The potentially motivating power of an education for humanization and its impact for students of color to determine the purpose for studying is captured by Leon's following statement:

It's self-stimulating, you know, to be in a classroom and find out like basically what's happening in the world. *It's not so much you doing it for a grade.* You doing it for yourself. You know what I'm saying? You really wanna know. It spark your interests. So, I'm basically doing it for myself. Like, it gets to the point where if it's an essay I'm assigned, in the past, I probably felt like I was doing my essay just to get a grade. Now if I'm writing an essay, I feel like I'm writing for a reason. Or for a cause.

Studying for self-determination enables those who are at the behest of ghetto schooling and structural violence to define their own learning outcomes. Engaging in learning that helps students demystify their oppression is important for students because it offers them concrete, historical ways to explain their current condition as oppressed people. Self-determination is infectious in that it has the power to transform reactionary politics and self-defeating resistance in others. Cultivating the attitude and mindset of helping others see the bigger picture helps set collective goals to overcome oppression. Students' ability to impact others in this way defines, in part, achievement from a humanizing educational perspective. Using what they learn to disrupt dehumanization is part of the process of self-determination as the learners define for themselves the purpose of learning.

So as not to romanticize the potential of humanization in this context, I must state that Leon did not transition easily out of the street life. He transferred to a continuation school after the semester because he was behind in credits. He did, however, continue to attend our class, as well as tutoring, in order to maintain a connection to the space and learning, even as an unenrolled student. Leon even applied to colleges the same way that other students were required to do so in our class. As a result of much advocacy, Leon was accepted into a state university in Northern California despite his low 1.6 cumulative GPA. After six years, Leon graduated from the university with a 3.2 GPA with a double major in communication studies and Africana studies.

To gain additional context, it's also important to understand the different life outcomes of Leon's closest friends. Around the time that Leon was finishing his first-semester final examinations in college, four of his friends were arrested—and eventually convicted—for a felony crime. After sentencing, two of his friends served six years, another served eight years, and his closest friend is currently finishing a minimum fifteen-year sentence. Three of his other friends were also convicted of felony charges; they were found guilty within one year of turning eighteen. Out of his nine closest friends, the only two who did not go to jail were Leon and his friend Xavier, who Leon insisted move with him to Northern California as his support system while he began his college years.

Upon my recently sharing with Leon the writing of this chapter, he elaborated, "I was the ringleader. I would have definitely went to jail if I didn't end up in college." For some time, Leon felt conflicted about his role in the community. He maintained close contact with friends in prison and felt a sense of guilt for having left them to pursue postsecondary education away from the community to which he was deeply connected. Today, although Leon is not using his education and street-informed leadership qualities to benefit the good of his community as an activist, he is gainfully employed, earning a six-figure salary managing a staff at a medical marijuana company in Northern California.

Relevant and Humanizing

Leon's understanding of education more than a decade after the time period described in the previous section and after having graduated from college effectively captures the contradiction related to SEL that is not critically relevant or humanizing:

> Coming up, we didn't value education because it was a dirty word. "Education is just a bunch of lies," that's what we think. No one is really trying to further their education. You never have a plan to go to college. School is just some shit you wake up and gotta do. . . If it wasn't for school, I couldn't dream the way I have. My dreams would be limited if I wasn't into learning and teaching myself, and always trying to improve.

Humanization involves opportunities through which students learn about and understand social issues in ways that resonate with their deeply intimate and often hostile experiences of life on the margins, using the humanity, skills, and brilliance they already bring to the classroom as a foundation for all learning.

Humanization as a critically relevant, and real, form of social and emotional health and well-being must channel the hurt and desire of students to express the pathos of community suffering that too often goes unacknowledged. As both an instructional practice and learning outcome, humanization is a political gesture by teachers to express, either implicitly or explicitly, that they understand the intimate burdens on our students' hopes, dreams, and desires. To state this outright is to indict and critique society, and to make scathing analysis of oppression essential to their healing and humanization.

To help the young people who experience dehumanization do the important work of humanization, consistently put students in positions to do the following:

- Engage in critical dialogue
- Study in the interests of their communities
- Be assessed on the compassion and leadership necessary to reframe ideologies used to rationalize hegemony

This, in essence, is *real social and emotional learning.*

KEY TAKEAWAYS

- SEL is color-blind and ahistorical, and thus does not ensure humanization.
- By contrast, humanization—knowledge of self, solidarity, and self-determination—addresses the real social and emotional needs of historically multiply marginalized students.
- To develop knowledge of self, students of color must learn to examine, explain, and interpret the world from their own perspectives.
- To build solidarity, teachers should develop their students' ideological clarity, build a sense of community based on this clarity, and hold one another accountable to a common, justice-centered purpose.
- Education as a practice of humanization uses the humanity, ways of knowing, and brilliance students already bring to the classroom as a foundation for all learning, especially to disrupt the dehumanization of institutionally imposed self-hate, divide-and-conquer approaches, and suboppression.

Questions from the Field

In our conversations with teachers, very important questions regarding social and emotional learning (SEL) arise. The following are a few that I hope are helpful in your work with students.

1. *What is the process for being vulnerable and engaged with humanization, first with oneself, then with one's pedagogy?*
    Teachers must first learn to be loving, introspective, and critically productive with their own selves before learning to incorporate this type of teaching and learning with their students. Examining their own process of engaging in knowledge of self and self-love can provide educators personal insights that can then inform their professional practice as classroom teachers. Teachers, then, must model the type of vulnerability that humanization requires to set

the tone for their students and to consider doing for themselves if inspired to do so on their own terms.

2. *In essence, many teachers do not really know much about people of color's experience, so why do these same teachers not take the time to get to know students on their own terms—instead of judging students based on teachers' own moral compasses?*

Given the demographics of the profession, many teachers often have the luxury to ignore how multiple marginalized students experience intersecting systems of oppression. This unfamiliarity with students' realities often makes the experience of listening to them very uncomfortable, because teachers feel implicated in the way students articulate their experiences with oppression or privilege. Teachers must understand that students' indictment of oppression is less about their feelings about their teachers as individuals and more about students' desire to feel listened to, respected, and supported in their pursuit to transform unjust social conditions. Doing otherwise reproduces ideologies that are at odds with the history and dignity of their students and their communities.

3. *How can teachers cultivate allies in their school community so that humanization is not just countercultural to otherwise bad teaching? Similarly, how can teachers protect themselves if they receive backlash from centering humanization with their students?*

Teachers who are interested in education for humanization in schooling contexts that normalize dehumanization must connect, first and foremost, with relatively like-minded individuals at their sites. These individuals should engage in activities that help them understand one another's purposes and, based on their sharing, come up with points of unity to which they are willing to commit their allegiances to one another. Exercises that increase their understanding of one another's experiences and identities will in turn build a stronger sense of community and allyship. Their collective understanding of social transformation generally, and of humanization specifically, will help them define the work ahead for them as justice-centered teachers looking to normalize these aims at their schools, beyond their individual classrooms. From here, this relatively small collective must identify, recruit, and support additional open-minded teachers who are willing to commit to the type of professional and political growth necessary to transform ineffective teaching in their own practices and the collective practice of their school. Committing to this type of collectivizing and service to students and community can help increase their influence over other teachers who may not even be interested in this process at all.

Recommended Resources

The readings in this section are categorized by topic, and it is recommended that you approach them in the order in which they appear.

Addressing Socially Toxic Stressors in Education

Duncan-Andrade, J.M.R. (2009). Note to educators: Hope required when growing roses in concrete. *Harvard Educational Review, 79,* **181–194.** This article made a fundamental impact on my recent scholarship as the first of its kind to link socially just education and research in the health sciences to advocate that teachers of students of color take on the added responsibility of reducing the negative health outcomes of students who are confronted with social stressors.

Ginwright, S. (2015). *Hope and healing in urban education.* **New York, NY: Routledge.** Ginwright draws on ethnographic case studies from community-based organizations and schools across the country to posit that radical healing and well-being require relational hope, restorative hope, and political hope.

Hammond, Z. L. (2014). *Culturally responsive teaching and the brain: Promoting authentic engagement and rigor among culturally and linguistically diverse students.* **Thousand Oaks, CA: Corwin Press.** Hammond draws on neuroscience and other brain-based research to inform teachers about more holistic approaches to culturally relevant teaching and learning.

Health Sciences and Social Connections

Perry, B. D., & Szalavitz, M. (2006). *The boy who was raised as a dog: And other stories from a child psychiatrist's notebook—What traumatized children can teach us about loss, love, and healing.* New York, NY: Basic Books. Perry, a child psychologist, and Szalavitz, a journalist who specializes in health and science, draw on cutting-edge medical research to analyze different case studies that have far-reaching implications for teachers whose youth experience socially toxic and traumatic stress.

Psychology of Oppression, Liberation, and Interpersonal Relationships

Moane, G. (2011). *Gender and colonialism: A psychological analysis of oppression and liberation.* New York, NY: Palgrave Macmillan. Moane draws on writings on colonialism, feminist psychology, liberation psychology, and psychological aspects of multiple oppressive dimensions to offer practical suggestions for mediating conflicts and perceived differences among subordinated people.

Howard, T. C. (2002). Hearing footsteps in the dark: African American students' descriptions of effective teachers. *Journal of Education for Students Placed at Risk, 7,* 425–444. Howard observed positive impacts on student effort, increased engagement with course content, and improved academic achievement when teachers (1) established community, family, and home-like characteristics, and (2) cultivated culturally connected caring relationships with students of color.

Szalavitz, M., & Perry, B. D. (2010). *Born for love: Why empathy is essential—and endangered.* New York, NY: HarperCollins. Szalavitz and Perry make profound connections between early developmental factors, intersectional identities, and neuroscience to examine how race and socioeconomic status affect empathy; they offer tangible suggestions to foster empathy, and reinforce the importance of connecting with and understanding others in our everyday relationships.

8

Helping the Unseen
Providing Educational Equity for Students Experiencing Homelessness

EARL J. EDWARDS

Homelessness is one of the most critical social issues impacting children and families throughout the United States. Although the economy has improved dramatically since the Great Recession in 2008, the number of K–12 students impacted by homelessness has steadily increased from 590,000 students to over 1.3 million. In major cities, towns, suburbs, and rural communities across the United States, a once unseen student population is now a visibly large subpopulation. Today, it's critical that school leaders and teachers understand and respond to the unique challenges faced by students experiencing homelessness, meanwhile continuing to develop competencies around critical wellness and implementing social-emotional learning in classrooms.

This chapter has three primary goals, the first of which is to raise awareness of the growing number of students experiencing homelessness in public schools throughout the United States and of its impact on academic achievement. Second, this chapter seeks to equip teachers and school leaders with the knowledge and strategies necessary to ensure that all students—stably housed or unstably housed—have access to the types of high-quality learning experiences in school that help them thrive. Third, the chapter discusses the federal policy designed to support students experiencing homelessness.

The Rise of Students Impacted by Homelessness

Student homelessness is a major issue in schools throughout the United States. Figure 8.1 shows that the number of students identified as homeless

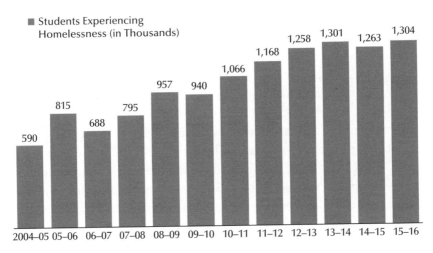

FIGURE 8.1   The Number of US Public School Students Experiencing Homelessness, 2004–2017

Sources: Child Trends. (2019). *Children and youth experiencing homelessness.* Retrieved from www. childtrends.org/indicators/homeless-children-and-youth

in US public schools has increased by 121 percent in the last twelve years, from 590,000 students to over 1.3 million.

In New York City Public Schools, the largest school district in the country, 1 in every 10 students is experiencing homelessness.[1] Similarly, major cities such as Los Angeles and Chicago have among the largest populations of students experiencing homelessness in the country. The large number of youth experiencing homelessness impacts more than urban districts; it significantly impacts suburban, town, and rural districts as well. Data from the National Center for Education Statistics shows that the likelihood of a student experiencing homelessness in a rural, suburban, or town district is virtually the same as that in an urban school district.[2] Given the high probability of encountering students experiencing homelessness in public schools across the country, it's imperative that educators understand what it means it be homeless and the different forms it can take.

HUD and the McKinney-Vento Homeless Assistance Act

Homeless is a term often used casually to refer to individuals who literally do not have shelter. The federal government, however, has operationalized and codified the term *homeless* through policies and legislation. The federal government has two different definitions of homeless, both of which align with specific agencies and federal resources. The US Department of Housing and Urban Development (HUD) defines homeless as a lack of a fixed, regular, and adequate nighttime residence. HUD focuses specifically on individuals who reside in (1) an emergency shelter or (2) a place not meant for human habitation, or (3) on individuals exiting an institution (i.e., prison, foster care group home, hospital) where he or she temporarily resided (42 U.S.C. 11302). Individuals or families that meet these criteria qualify for federal support, such as Section 8 housing vouchers, rapid rehousing subsidies, and permanent supportive housing. In addition, states and local municipalities have aligned their definition of homeless with the federal government in order to enhance funding for their local efforts.

The definition used by HUD, however, is adult centric. Schools and institutions specifically focused on supporting youth use a different definition under the federal McKinney-Vento Homeless Assistance Act. The McKinney-Vento Act, which is mandated to provide funding for homeless shelter programs, defines homeless youth as follows:

1. Children and youths who are sharing the housing of other persons due to loss of housing, economic hardship, or a similar reason (also referred to as being "doubled up")
2. Children and youths who have a primary nighttime residence that is a public or private place not designed for or ordinarily used as a regular sleeping accommodation for human beings
3. Children and youths who are living in cars, parks, public spaces, abandoned buildings, substandard housing, bus or train stations, or similar settings
4. Migratory children who qualify as homeless because they are children who are living in similar circumstances listed in points 1–3 (42 U.S.C. 11431)

This policy's definition of youth homelessness dramatically expands on HUD's definition, as it includes youth who are forced to share housing with others due to economic hardship.[3] Because doubled-up families are not included in the HUD definition of homelessness, HUD does not provide them with resources. This is extremely important for educators to know, as 76 percent of students who are homeless in schools are doubled up and likely do not qualify for federal, state, city, and county support aligned with HUD's definition of homelessness.[4] The lack of awareness of the McKinney-Vento Act's definition of homelessness puts those who are doubled up at greater risk of being unidentified and undersupported.

In addition to defining student homelessness, the McKinney-Vento Act is the most comprehensive federal legislation designed to support the academic achievement of students impacted by homelessness. The policy mandates that once students are identified as experiencing homelessness, schools are legally responsible for ensuring that their homeless conditions do not interfere with their ability to access a quality education comparable to that of their stable-housed peers. The policy can be used to mitigate any inequity for students experiencing homelessness, and it explicitly calls out the following rights:

- **Access to school.** All students experiencing homelessness have the right and discretion either to stay at their current school or to immediately enroll in the public school closest to their relocation. If students live far away from their current school, the district is required to provide transportation. Furthermore, unstable housing should not prohibit students' participation in afterschool programs and enrichment activities.
- **Access to food.** All students experiencing homelessness are immediately enrolled in free breakfast and lunch programs at school.
- **Academic support.** All students experiencing homelessness are eligible for academic tutoring and enrichment programs provided by the school to ensure that they are able to access the mainstream curriculum.
- **Homeless liaison.** Each state and local education agency is required to have at least one liaison with the responsibility of identifying students experiencing homelessness, and upholding the actualization of the policy.

Although the McKinney-Vento Act specifies these rights, implementing the policy is still a challenge for many school districts.[5] Currently, districts are only required to have one homeless liaison for all of its schools. As the only person responsible for carrying out the mandates of the policy at each school site, the homeless liaison is often severely overworked and oftentimes fulfilling several additional roles within the school district.[6] Many homeless liaisons only have time to focus on administrative mandates of the act and little time to provide students with tutoring opportunities, counseling, and resources for community programming.[7] In addition, many homeless liaisons struggle to reach a large percentage of youth impacted by homelessness. This means that many of these students are either unidentified or receiving minimal support. Therefore, it's essential for school leaders, teachers, and other school staff to identify and support students experiencing homelessness.

The Different Living Contexts of Homelessness

As the McKinney-Vento Act recognizes, youth do not have to live on the street to be considered homeless. Homelessness has many contexts. And although all settings of homelessness are detrimental to children's academic and social outcomes, each poses unique challenges. For example, although doubling up offers adolescents experiencing homelessness with housing and the ability to disconnect from the stigma of experiencing homelessness, students in doubled-up homes have fewer educational and social opportunities than students in homeless shelters.[8] Because of this disparity, it's important for educators to be able to identify students who are doubled up and connect them to resources even when the students themselves may not identify as homeless.

Youth who live on the streets are more likely to be separated from their families, less likely to be enrolled in school, and more likely to abuse substances and battle depression.[9] They're also less likely to receive educational and social opportunities than youth experiencing homelessness in emergency shelters.

Experiencing homelessness as a family also has a unique set of stressors. Families living in family shelters, for example, are forced to adjust their family routines and face additional scrutiny and surveillance.[10] Homeless shelters typically have strict rules about food, discipline, and chores that families are required to follow, even though those rules may undermine effective parenting practices. Many parents feel that their parenting styles are watched closely and that if they do not follow the shelter rules, they'll be asked to leave or lose their children to foster care. The eroding of parental control increases parents' level of toxic stress and in turn decreases parents' ability to mitigate their children's stress. Exposure to such stress can have negative psychological and academic consequences for youth. Table 8.1 describes some of the different living

TABLE 8.1   Common Living Contexts for Students Experiencing Homelessness

Living Conditions	Description	Percentage of Homeless Population (2015–16 SY)	Challenges
Doubled up	When a family (or student) is forced to temporarily live with another family due to loss of permanent housing	76	• There is limited access to federal and state housing programs. • Students live in overcrowded spaces. • Students endure high levels of toxic stress as a result of conflict between parent and adult host.
Living in a shelter or transitional housing.	When a family (or student) is living in a transitional housing program due to loss of permanent housing	14	• Cities and towns have a limited number of family shelters, and some students have long commutes to school. • Family shelters have strict curfews, which could impact students' ability to attend extracurricular activities.
Sleeping in motels/hotels	When a family (or student) is living in a motel for interim housing due to loss of permanent housing	7	• A typical motel has only a microwave, which prevents families from eating substantive and healthy meals. • Families living in motel rooms are often overcrowded and tend not to have a quiet space for students to do homework.
Living on the streets	When a family (or student) has no consistent shelter and sleeps in public spaces	3	• Students are less likely to attend school due to the stress and energy exerted for basic survival. • Students tend not to have access to showers, food, or other basic necessities.

(Continued)

TABLE 8.1 *(Continued)*

Living Conditions	Description	Percentage of Homeless Population (2015–16 SY)	Challenges
Living in a car or RV	When a family (or student) has no consistent shelter and is living in a car or RV		• Living in a car provides more physical safety than living on the street.
Unaccompanied minors	Youth who are not in the physical custody of a parent or guardian	9	• Unaccompanied minors are likely to have minimal adult support and advocacy. In addition to navigating school, they may also be navigating shelters and social services offices alone.

conditions of students experiencing homelessness. The percentage total in Table 8.1 does not equal 100 percent because a student can be identified as a unaccompanied minor while also residing in one of the other living conditions.

The Psychological and Academic Impact of Homelessness

Enduring homelessness is a prolonged traumatic experience that often produces high levels of toxic stress for children and youth and directly affects their critical wellness. The National Scientific Council on the Developing Child defines **toxic stress** as severe, frequent, and/or extended activation of the body's sympathetic nervous system.[11] The sympathetic nervous system, responsible for what is commonly known as the fight-or-flight response, regulates the body's severe stress response. Normally, the sympathetic nervous system produces stress hormones to increase the body's ability to address immediate physical harm, while lowering the brain's cognitive activity. Although this hormonal process is natural, when the sympathetic nervous system continues to produce stress hormones for extended periods of time, the hormones reach toxic levels and can have long-term effects on a child's body and cognitive development.[12]

Toxic stress can make it difficult for students experiencing homelessness to concentrate in school. Moreover, students enduring toxic stress may be hypersensitive, irritable, and tired in class.[13] Teachers often misidentify symptoms of toxic stress as disengagement, defiance, or a cognitive disability. Although some students experiencing homelessness may have a learning disability, many are misdiagnosed and placed in special education courses.[14]

The National Center for Homeless Education reports that 60 percent of students experiencing homelessness perform below grade level in state reading (ELA) assessments, and 75 percent perform below grade level in math.[15] National data also shows that these students have lower rates of high school completion.[16] Adolescents who leave high school before graduating are introduced to a new host of negative outcomes as adults. For example, adults without high school diplomas have unemployment rates nearly twice that of the average US worker and earn substantially less money over their lifetime when compared to high school graduates.[17] As a result, when homeless youth fail to complete high school, the likelihood of their experiencing homelessness as adults increases.

Student Mobility

Another significant barrier to the academic achievement is a phenomenon referred to as student mobility, the frequent transferring between schools within one academic school year. Within one school year, 41 percent of students experiencing homelessness will attend two schools, and 28 percent will attend three or more.[18] Further, families experiencing homelessness are forced to move unexpectedly with very little time for planning. In many cases, families experiencing homelessness are moving from a permanent location to a temporary one. This causes high levels of uncertainty and anxiety for students and their families because they're already thinking about their next move. In addition, students are forced to acclimate to a new school. Adjusting to a new school culture, acclimating to new teacher expectations, creating new friendships, all while attempting to catch up on previously taught materials, can be extremely difficult.

Chronic Absenteeism

Chronic absenteeism is a particularly significant challenge for students experiencing homelessness. Many school districts define chronic absenteeism as missing more than 10 percent (about eighteen school days) of an academic year. Chronic absenteeism dramatically affects the academic achievement of students at all grade levels.[19] In an attempt to maintain stability, students experiencing homelessness may travel far in order to stay at their school of origin. The long commutes can often cause them to be tardy to school. For schools with static class schedules, a student experiencing homelessness may miss 10 percent of his or her first-period class due to tardiness. In addition, families attempting to receive housing services are often required to bring their children with them to the meetings. Because these local and federal government offices typically close at 5 p.m., students are forced either to miss school entirely or to arrive late.[20]

To truly apply a critical wellness framework in their classrooms or schools, educators must understand the academic impact that toxic stress, school mobility, and chronic absenteeism have on students experiencing homelessness. Being aware of these barriers enables educators to empathize with students and, more important, create strategies to mitigate the negative effects of such barriers. In addition, it's important for educators to understand not only the challenges these students face but also which groups of youths are most vulnerable. Table 8.2 lists behaviors that may be signs that a student is homeless.

Students Most at Risk for Homelessness

Youth homelessness is a devastating epidemic with negative outcomes for students across all racial demographics. With this in mind, there are some student populations with a higher risk of becoming homeless: Black students, Latinx students, and LGBT students. To better understand this increased risk, let's take a closer look at each population.

Black Students

Black students are disproportionately affected by homelessness. Although they make up only 14 percent of American families, Black families represent 49 percent of all families living in homeless shelters.[21] African Americans are three times more likely to be homeless than any other racial group. High levels of systemic racism make Black families particularly susceptible to homelessness. Hiring discrimination, employment discrimination, and the substandard education provided to Black youth in school create a perfect storm for housing instability.[22]

TABLE 8.2.   Potential Signs That a Student May Be Experiencing Homelessness

Behavior	Rationale for Behavior
Abnormal tiredness in class	Students lack privacy. They are sleeping on living room couches, in overcrowded shelters, in high-traffic motels, or in public spaces that are not conducive to sleeping.
Abrupt increase in tardiness or absenteeism	Students in temporary residences are often far from their school. Students are forced to wake up earlier and travel longer to get to school. The longer commute can result in more tardiness and decrease students' motivation for attending. Further, students miss school in order to attend meetings to receive housing support.
Disengagement from school activities	Students may stay in a shelter or with another family that requires them to come to their residence earlier. In addition, the longer commute to school could force students to leave school immediately in order to make their curfew.
Shift in behaviors, increased outbursts during class, or increased irritability	Students often experience a lot of toxic stress. When they do not feel comfortable or do not have the opportunity to express their feelings in a productive way, they may release their stress through misbehaving in school.

Latinx Students

Latinx students are significantly impacted by homelessness, especially in states with large Latinx populations. In Texas, Latinx students made up 52 percent of the general population and 48 percent of the student homeless population in the 2017-18 school year.[23] Similar trends are found in New York, Florida, and California. Further, despite their large numbers, Latinx students are the most likely to be undercounted due to fear of government authorities.[24] Enrolling in shelters or speaking with school officials about housing issues becomes especially dangerous for recent immigrants—both documented or undocumented—who fear deportation.

LGBT Students

Lesbian, gay, bisexual, and transgender (LGBT) youth represent another demographic of students disproportionately affected by homelessness. LGBT youth make up 30 to 40 percent of clients served by homeless youth agencies, dropout centers, and outreach and housing programs,[25] and they are twice as likely to experience homelessness as heterosexual youth.[26] LGBT students tend to be homeless as a result of running away from their families or being forced out by their families due to their sexual orientation.[27] LGBT youth who experience homelessness are at higher risk for mental health issues, substance abuse, and suicidal thoughts as compared to heterosexual adolescents who experience homelessness.

Supporting Students Experiencing Homelessness

In addition to raising their own awareness of the McKinney-Vento Homeless Assistance Act, teachers can do a lot to support students experiencing homelessness. The following sections describe six principles schools can utilize to improve the educational opportunities for students experiencing homelessness. Principles 1 through 3 can be implemented at the classroom level; Principles 4 through 6 require a whole-school approach. For each of the principles, I have included strategies for implementation.

Principle 1: Attend to Students' Basic Needs

Students cannot excel in school if their basic needs are not met. Maslow's hierarchy of needs highlights that an individual's basic necessities, such as food, water, rest, and safety, must be met before he or she is capable of prioritizing any other task. As a community of educators, we must make sure that students' basic needs are covered when they enter our schools. The following are some strategies for implementing this principle.

Strategy 1: Open Your Classroom for Breakfast and Lunch

Even though all students experiencing homelessness have access to food at school, they may not be eating it. In some schools, eating the free lunch is seen as humiliating and some students (including students experiencing homelessness) would rather stay hungry than eat school meals in front of their peers. An effective solution for middle and high schools could be to offer students the opportunity to eat lunch in your classroom. The classroom could provide students a place to eat without being judged. This also gives the teacher a chance to build an authentic relationship with the student. Although teachers may not want to open up their classroom every day during lunch, they can coordinate with another teacher so that students have several classrooms to go to in order to eat in peace.

Strategy 2: Create a Resource Room

Another strategy teachers and school leaders could utilize is to create a resource room for all students at their school. Students experiencing homelessness (especially those unhoused) may have limited access to clothes and hygiene products. A resource room in an accessible location will enable students to discreetly take what they need. The supplies can be donated by parents or local businesses, and the school district homeless liaison could support the initiative. Teachers could also make a "resource corner" in their classrooms where students can take what they need. Although there may be an inclination to exclude students in stable housing from taking resources, it's important that everyone is invited to take what he or she needs. Being labeled homeless is stigmatizing, and being forced to disclose your housing status to receive resources could prevent the neediest students from utilizing the support.

Principle 2: Create a Supportive Environment

School is one of few places many students can feel safe. Unfortunately for many kids experiencing homelessness, school becomes another unsafe space. A national survey of students who experienced homelessness found that only 45 percent of them felt that their school did an adequate job of providing them with emotional support.[28] Establishing a strong relationship with a caring adult at school not only provides students with the opportunity to feel safe but also can lower students' toxic stress.[29] Here are a couple of strategies for creating a supportive environment.

Strategy 1: Use Class Assignments as a Relationship-Building Tool

One strategy for creating a safe space for students within your classroom is to use assignments as an opportunity to learn more about your students. A common practice in middle and high schools is to use a quick five- to eight-minute individual assignment at the start of class called a "Do Now." Typically, teachers use a Do Now to review previously taught content or to introduce the upcoming unit. Teachers can, however, dedicate a weekly Do Now assignment to check in with their students. The assignment could be as simple as asking, "How was your weekend?" or "Who do you consider to be a role model?"

Although Do Nows do not have to be graded, they should be responded to either verbally or in writing. For example, if a student shares that he went to the movies over the weekend, a teacher could simply ask about the movie when she sees the student in the hall between classes. Such interactions may seem miniscule, but over time they demonstrate to students that teachers care about their lives beyond the classroom. As students get used to responding to the Do Now activity and start to trust their teacher, they may use the activity as an opportunity to seek help.

Strategy 2: Model Honesty and Vulnerability

Although providing students with the opportunity to share their personal lives in the classroom is important, teachers' being honest and vulnerable with students is critical for establishing a safe space for students experiencing homelessness. Teachers' sharing their authentic selves in the classroom is important for two critical reasons. First, willingness to share challenges, strengths, and goals helps humanize teachers. Too often, students only see teachers as people who teach a specific subject or discipline them. This limited perspective prevents students from connecting with their teachers. Second, teachers can use their challenges as models for how students can tackle their own problems. For example, teachers can share a current or past struggle that they were able to get through with the help and support of others. The point of sharing vulnerable moments is not to belittle students' challenges but rather to normalize the need for help. Although this strategy doesn't explicitly target students experiencing homelessness, it does help create a space where they can feel comfortable and safe.

Principle 3: Provide Effective Instruction

Although students experiencing homelessness have a lot to overcome outside of school, this does not mean that teachers should lower their academic expectations. Many of these students aspire to graduate high school, attend college, and pursue a career helping those who are disenfranchised.[30] The majority of students who experience homelessness, however, feel that their school is not doing a good job of supporting them academically.[31] Schools must ensure that students are receiving a rigorous education that pushes them to be college and career ready. To help provide effective instruction, consider the following strategies.

Strategy 1: De-Emphasize the Role of Attendance in Grading

As mentioned earlier, absenteeism and tardiness are significant challenges for students experiencing homelessness. Some school grading policies are structured in a way that punishes students for being absent rather than assessing what a student actually learned. Consider this typical grade breakdown for a high school or middle school class:

- 10 percent for homework (late homework only accepted for students with excused absences)
- 10 percent for attendance
- 25 percent for class work
- 15 percent for quizzes
- 30 percent for tests
- 10 percent for the final exam

This breakdown may seem fair, but it puts students experiencing homelessness (or other vulnerable students) at a disadvantage. Missing a day of school could potentially cause a student to lose considerable points, and it makes it very difficult for a student experiencing homelessness who has mastered the content to receive a high grade. Once students feel that their grades are not matching their acquired knowledge and effort, they may disengage and voluntarily skip school, thereby exacerbating their attendance issue.

Using a grading system that de-emphasizes attendance and focuses on the content that students have learned provides students experiencing homelessness with the flexibility to obtain strong grades in school and stay motivated in their learning. Systems such as mastery learning, project-based learning, and problem-based learning focus on mastery milestones and the creation of a final product that demonstrates learning objectives.

Strategy 2: Host Study Halls within Your Department or Grade

For students doubling up, living in motels, residing in a car, or living on the streets, one of the most difficult barriers is simply having a safe and quiet place to do homework. Teachers and schools can mitigate this by implementing department- or grade-level study halls. Teachers can rotate the responsibility of hosting study halls for their students in order to lessen the workload.

Although the study hall space is meant to provide students with the opportunity to do their homework, it should not take the form of a traditional classroom. Instead, it should be modeled after something closer to a café. Students should feel free to listen to music and casually talk with their peers without fear of getting into trouble. Once students feel safe in the space, the study hall will become a desirable location to do work and receive academic support. The study hall can become a hub for tutoring and a space to retake quizzes or exams.

Principle 4: Use a Multilevel Approach to Provide Resources to Students Experiencing Homelessness

Coordinating resources to identify and support students experiencing homelessness is a serious challenge. The expectation that one homeless liaison in the district will be able to adequately support hundreds, or even thousands, of students across dozens of schools is impractical. In order to adequately support the academic and social emotional needs of students experiencing homelessness, there must be strategic coordination among the school district, staff, and faculty at school and families impacted by homelessness. Following is a useful strategy for implementing this principle.

Strategy 1: Establish a Comprehensive McKinney-Vento Team

The strategy for this principle is straightforward: each school should design its own McKinney-Vento team that considers and monitors the needs of unstably housed students and their families. In addition to the district homeless liaison, the ideal McKinney-Vento team would include a school homeless liaison, school administrator, school counselor, student and family liaison, and one of the student's current teachers. Each person on the team should be fully aware of the McKinney-Vento Homeless Assistance Act. In addition, the student and family should be able to talk with anyone on the team to get connected with resources.

Principle 5: Raise Awareness of the McKinney-Vento Homeless Assistance Act

One of the most challenging barriers to supporting students experiencing homelessness is that many teachers, students, and parents from schools across the district have never heard of the policy. This means that they don't know the rights of students experiencing homelessness. Ensuring that all stakeholders are aware of the McKinney-Vento Homeless Assistance Act and its definition of student homelessness and that they know how to access the appropriate person for additional resources is paramount to successfully supporting students experiencing homelessness. The following are two strategies to help implement this principle.

Strategy 1: Provide Professional Development for All Staff

All faculty and staff should have at least one professional development (PD) session that is dedicated to addressing student homelessness. The PD should cover the following: (1) defining student homelessness, (2) identifying the district's homeless liaison, and (3) explaining the explicit rights of students experiencing homelessness as stated in the McKinney-Vento Homeless Assistance Act. This PD session should include all staff members, but especially teachers, front office staff, administrators, deans, coaches, lunch staff, after-school coordinators, parent liaisons, counselors, and resource officers. These are people who interact with students daily and could play vital roles in identifying students experiencing homelessness and directing them to resources. Although I recommend one PD for the whole staff, strategies for supporting students experiencing homelessness should be part of the school's ongoing PD.

Strategy 2: Publicize the McKinney-Vento Homeless Assistance Act on the School Website

Although information on the McKinney-Vento Homeless Assistance Act can be found on state- and district-level websites, it's often missing from local school websites. Because homelessness is a stigmatized experience, students and parents may not want to attempt to research resources on their own. The family may have limited experience interacting with the district website and naturally go to their school's website for information. Unfortunately, many families take the lack of information provided as a sign that support doesn't exist. A simple solution is to ensure that your school website defines student homelessness, identifies the district's homeless liaison, and explains the explicit rights for students experiencing homelessness stated in the McKinney-Vento Homeless Assistance Act. When parents and students have the autonomy to research student homelessness information on their own and see the benefits of disclosing their housing instability, they'll be more likely to disclose their homeless status to their school and receive assistance that can make a significant difference in a student's life.

Principle 6: Use Data to Identify and Respond to Subpopulations of Students Experiencing Homelessness

Acknowledging students experiencing homelessness as a vulnerable population is a very important first step. The next step is to identify potential disparities between subpopulations within a homeless group. Homelessness can impact students differently depending on their living conditions and their race, gender, and sexual orientation. To help identify subpopulations experiencing homelessness, consider this strategy.

Strategy 1: Disaggregate Data for Students Experiencing Homelessness

Figure 8.2 uses data from New York City Public Schools as an illustration of a potentially hidden homeless subpopulation.

The aggregated suspension data shows that 3.2 percent of students experiencing homelessness in city schools in the 2015–16 school year were suspended, just 1 percentage point less than the typical low-income students in the district. If a school is making data-informed decisions, it is unlikely to prioritize suspension as a problem that needs to be addressed for students experiencing homelessness. When you disaggregate the suspension data for students experiencing homelessness by race, however, it reveals that Black students experiencing homelessness have the highest suspension rates among all students. This second level of data analysis makes

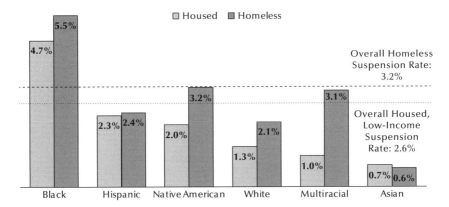

FIGURE 8.2   New York City Public Schools Suspension Rates, by Housing Status and Race/ Ethnicity (2015–16 SY)

Source: Adapted from Institute for Children, Poverty & Homelessness. *On the map: The atlas of student homelessness in New York City 2017.* Retrieved from www.icphusa.org/reports/map-atlas-student-homelessness-new-york-city-2017/

visible a subpopulation that was previously unseen. Once vulnerable sub-populations are identified, interventions can be designed to specifically support their needs.

Homelessness is a national crisis with a direct impact on students' ability to succeed. Although schools cannot stop the root causes of homelessness, they can make sure that homeless conditions do not rob children of the opportunity to achieve in school. Educators who are aware of student homelessness and are ready to support one of our nation's most vulnerable student populations will ensure that all students receive a high-quality education no matter their living conditions.

What Would You Do?

To gain some clarity with regard to the challenges of student homelessness, consider the following scenarios for thought and discussion.

Scenario 1: You are a sixth-grade teacher, and your colleague Ms. Nuñez shares her concern that one of her students may be homeless. She reads you one of that student's essays, which says that his mom and aunt decided to split rent and get an apartment together. The student shares that he is stressed because he is leaving the house he grew up in and will now have to share a room with his older cousin.

Consider the following questions:

1. Is Ms. Nuñez's student experiencing homelessness according to the McKinney-Vento Homeless Assistance Act?
2. Ms. Nuñez wants to respond to her student; how should she approach the issue?
3. Should Ms. Nuñez call her student's parent? If yes, what should she say?

Scenario 2: After arriving to your first-period class fifteen minutes late for the tenth time, one of your ninth-grade students privately discloses that she and her father are living in motels. The motels are far from school, and she has to wait for her dad to get off after his second shift of work for him to drive her to school. She could take the local bus; however, her father told her that the situation will be temporary, and he is adamantly saving all of his money for an apartment.

Although you are the only person she disclosed to, there are rumors that she is staying at a motel across town. A twelfth-grade teacher does not know the student, but heard the rumors and asked you whether they are true.

Consider the following questions:

1. How should you respond to your colleague?
2. How would you go about helping your student and her father?
3. The father refuses to identify as homeless. How could you convince him to disclose?

Scenario 3: You have a tenth-grade Black student named Jacob in your chemistry class who has been identified by your school district as homeless. Although Jacob is passing your class with an A, he is failing all of his other core courses. If Jacob does not pass his classes this semester, there is a strong possibility that he will have to repeat the eleventh grade. Empathizing with the stress Jacob is enduring, your colleagues want to remove his poor homework and class participation grades, and also allow him to retake the exams he failed. When you ask whether other students will have the same opportunity to improve their grades, they replied that they are making these modifications only for Jacob.

Consider the following questions:

1. Do you agree with your colleagues' decision? Why or why not?
2. Are there any additional strategies that could be used to help Jacob improve his grades?
3. Do you think anyone else should be invited into the conversation before the aforementioned modifications are made for Jacob?

KEY TAKEAWAYS

- Youth homelessness is a growing challenge facing schools today, and it is hindering the educational opportunities for students experiencing housing instability. If you teach in an urban, suburban, or rural school district, you are likely to be teaching students experiencing homelessness. All teachers and staff must develop the knowledge, skills, and awareness to best support students impacted by homelessness.
- The McKinney-Vento Homeless Assistance Act expands on the common definition of homelessness and includes students finding temporary housing by doubling up with another family. The policy also provides students experiencing homelessness with explicit rights in order to ensure the same access to education as their stably housed peers.
- To unlock the hidden potential of students experiencing homelessness, teachers and school leaders should (1) attend to students' basic needs, (2) create a supportive environment for students, (3) provide effective instruction, (4) establish a comprehensive McKinney-Vento team, (5) raise awareness about the McKinney-Vento Homeless Assistance Act, and (6) use data to identify and respond to subpopulations of students experiencing homelessness.

Questions from the Field

In our conversations with teachers, very important questions regarding students experiencing homelessness arise. The following are a few that I hope are helpful in your work with students.

1. *How can you tell whether a student is experiencing homelessness? Are there any signs?*

   Students experiencing homelessness do not have a look. In fact, students experiencing homelessness are often trying their absolute best not to stand out from their peers. However, sudden shifts in a student's behavior at school may be a sign that a student is experiencing housing instability. Four common shifts to look for are (1) abnormal tiredness in class, (2) a decrease in attendance, (3) sudden disengagement from class and/or extracurricular activities, and (4) increased irritability or number of outbursts in class. The four shifts are only observable, however, if school adults are building meaningful relationships with students and paying attention to their overall well-being.

2. *If I find out that a student is homeless, should I report it as neglect?*

   If you find out that a child is experiencing homelessness, you should not immediately assume that the child is being neglected by his or her parents or guardians. A financial crisis, natural disaster, family death, divorce, eviction, or a house fire are just a few examples of circumstances that could lead a child to lose stable housing, while still being in the custody of a caring and supportive adult. If you find out that a child is experiencing homelessness, notify your school district's homeless liaison. The liaison can meet with the student and the student's family to get a better understanding of the child's circumstance. Prematurely citing a family experiencing homelessness for neglect will break trust between that family and the school. Moreover, the incident will reverberate throughout the district and may prevent other families experiencing homelessness from disclosing and receiving resources.

3. *How do I convince students or parents to identify themselves as homeless to the district if they are hesitant to disclose?*

   Families often do not disclose their homeless status to the school district because (1) the family is fearful of being cited for neglect and (2) they do not think the school district will provide substantial help. If you want to convince parents and students to disclose their homeless status to the district, you have to make sure they fully understand their rights under the McKinney-Vento Homeless Assistance Act and that they are aware of all the material supports that students experiencing homelessness are qualified to receive. Once families are fully informed, they are more likely to disclose their homeless status to the school district.

4. *Should I start special clubs or groups specifically for homeless students?*

   I would not recommend starting a group specifically for students experiencing homelessness. Being considered homeless is stigmatizing, and many students would not join the club because they are unwilling to disclose their homeless status to a broad community. I would recommend that school districts actively recruit, enroll, and support students impacted by homelessness into well-established leadership and expanded learning opportunities. Such opportunities can keep students who are experiencing homelessness connected to school, meanwhile providing them with an opportunity to build agency and to lead.

Recommended Resources

BOOKS

Hallet, R. E., & Skrla, L. (2017). *Serving students who are homeless: A resource guide for schools, districts, and educational leaders.* **New York, NY: Teachers College Press.** Hallet and Skrla provide a district- and school-level approach to supporting students experiencing homelessness. This book will be helpful to school leaders who are ready to implement comprehensive, trauma-informed practices for students experiencing homelessness.

Aviles de Bradley, A. (2015). *From equity to charity: Race, homelessness, and urban schools.* **New York, NY: Teachers College Press.** Aviles de Bradley provides a critical analysis of racialized student homelessness. This book reveals the additional challenges that Black and Latinx students may face when experiencing homelessness in urban communities. This is a critical read for educators serving in low-income, urban communities of color.

ONLINE RESOURCES

National Center for Homeless Education (nche.ed.gov). The National Center for Homeless Education (NCHE) is the US Department of Education's technical assistance and information center for the federal Education for Homeless Children and Youth program. NCHE provides resources for educators serving students experiencing homelessness and briefs for how to best utilize the McKinney-Vento Homeless Assistance Act.

SchoolHouse Connection (schoolhouseconnection.org). SchoolHouse Connection is a national nonprofit working to overcome homelessness through raising awareness. The nonprofit hosts webinars with homeless liaisons and policy experts that keep educators informed on technical and concrete practices that support students experiencing homelessness.

Conclusion

Sustaining the Critical Wellness Approach

Over the past several years, there has been a groundswell of support by and for classroom teachers. Cities such as Los Angeles, Denver, and Oakland and states such as Arizona, West Virginia, and Oklahoma have witnessed strikes that have brought much-needed attention to the work of teachers. What has been clear in many of these movements is that the issues have not been solely about money but about resources to support students. In many states and districts across the country, teachers are calling for additional support for mental health and social emotional development. Teachers are demanding more counselors, nurses, and mental health therapists. In essence, teachers are making a call for local, district, state, and federal governments to recognize the damage that has been done to students by historical and institutional racism, divestments in communities, and structural inequities. In other words, teachers are telling local, state, and federal governments and the public that student learning will not be maximized until student social emotional wellness is a priority.

The authors of *All Students Must Thrive* believe that this social emotional wellness is essential for all students to thrive. What is clear throughout this work, however, is that placing the focus on academics as students' first priority is an approach that must be rethought. Student wellness and well-being are just as essential, if not more so, than academic well-being. In 1943, Abraham Maslow discussed his well-known hierarchy of needs. The framework remains as relevant today as it was almost eighty years ago. Student self-actualization is not likely to occur if basic needs such as health, safety, and social and emotional well-being are not tended to first.[1] The scholars in this book make a compelling case that in the twenty-first century, racial inequity, toxic stressors, homelessness, cultural invalidation, and the rendering invisible of nondominant populations contribute to the mental and emotional distress that many students encounter in schools. The school reform discourse is slowly shifting away from an incessant focus on accountability and mind-numbing test taking to one in which community schools are being discussed as a viable alternative.

The idea that schools must be attentive to the multiple layers of students' lives is not a radical one. Moreover, the idea that schools can and should play an instrumental role in supporting students and their families holistically is gaining important, and desperately needed, attention. To be clear, this effort to support all students—but in particular, the most vulnerable populations—requires a multilayered approach. Complex problems are not solved with simplistic or reductive solutions. Interventions at the macro level undoubtedly must serve as a catalyst for authentic and sustained transformation. There must be robust fiscal investments into our most economically disadvantaged neighborhoods and schools. School nurses, smaller classroom sizes, school counselors, and mental health workers need to be staples at every school, yet it often appears that districts with the most cumulative disadvantage are missing these basic school necessities.

This must change.

At the school level, leaders must be bold, courageous, and willing to challenge deficit mindsets. They must disrupt teacher apathy and seek to inspire a way to reimagine schools that is centered on equity, transformation, and humanization. Subsequently, classroom teachers must recognize that despite the odds that are seemingly stacked against them in the classroom, they are able to be change agents. Identifying and enhancing pedagogical approaches that are anchored in a critical wellness framework that seeks to disrupt racism, sexism, homophobia, colonialism, and xenophobia are essential. The cultivation of deeply caring and loving relationships between students and teachers can help build a platform for teaching and learning that is deeply rooted in demonstrating to students that they do matter, that their wellness is essential, and that they can thrive in their quest to learn. All students should experience schools that have developed rigorous, culturally meaningful approaches to instruction and content. Recognizing students' sociocultural realities outside of school can also communicate to students that teachers and school personnel can be supportive in ways that many students are not accustomed to, but truly deserve. These approaches must also be adopted by paraprofessionals, instructional coaches, college counselors, academic counselors, and classified staff. Such a transformative approach requires all stakeholders to be on board. To that end, partnering and engaging with parents and caregivers are essential to this work as well.

All Students Must Thrive is meant to help educators at all levels to reimagine schools and the education models that purport to enhance student development. In many ways, today's schools still remain steeped in a nineteenth-century model that no longer matches the needs of the twenty-first-century student population. Therefore, it is vital that we step outside of traditional approaches and undo the dehumanizing ways that particular students are told that their stories, their histories, their realities, their fears, and their dreams and aspirations do not matter.

If we are honest, we as a society continue to fall woefully short in supporting and educating large segments of our student population, in particular some of our most vulnerable student populations. To amend this shortfall, a *critical wellness* approach in education brings together three theoretical frameworks that have relevance for equity in schools: *wellness, critical pedagogy*, and *critical race theory*. The interlocking theoretical frames do not seek to offer a recipe, or how-to approach, to how we reimagine schools. To the contrary, these theoretical frames provide a structure through which the strategies and ideas in this book can be applied to schools and their given context. The approaches and interventions outlined in this work will manifest differently given the city, county, state, or district. Whether educators are in a small rural, large urban, or midsize suburban district, we believe that the principles outlined in this book are relevant and important. Whether the student population is largely socioeconomically disadvantaged, racially segregated, or a balanced mosaic from diverse backgrounds, this work is still pertinent.

Today's schools need strategic alliances and ecosystems of support that refuse to allow students to fall through the cracks. Society needs the development of schools where all personnel (certificated and classified) are equipped with knowledge, skills, dispositions, and resources to serve students in a myriad of ways. This means that schools need to become hubs of learning for children, youth, *and* adults. Learning that is child and community focused would be tied to a core belief around community-based assets, historical richness in neighborhoods, and the idea that all students with adequate and sustained support can reach their full potential.

It is also important for educators to understand and acknowledge the dramatic demographic transformations that are occurring nationwide.

The new normal that positions youth of color as the majority needs to be embraced and seen as a strength of our schools. Furthermore, the influx of new languages, new experiences, and new realities in our nation's schools provides avenues for learning for all stakeholders. What must be challenged, however, is the recalcitrant continuation of ethnic and racial segregation in our schools and neighborhoods. What has been abundantly clear is that far too many youth of color are concentrated in underfunded schools with inexperienced and underqualified educators. This has become a recipe for trauma and exclusion. Conversely, we must be aware of the experience of youth of color who attend predominantly White schools, and the toxic stress brought on by racial microaggressions, social exclusion, and academic marginalization on the part of peers and adults.

All Students Must Thrive also speaks to the challenges that are prevalent in our rural communities. Although these geographical areas are often absent from the conversation on school reform, we acknowledge the deep pockets of economic deprivation that exist in countless rural communities nationwide. The goal of helping all students thrive must take into account all of our most overlooked populations. To that end, this book remains deeply mindful of arguably our most forgotten school population, Indigenous populations that continue to suffer even on sovereign lands. The need to recognize the effects of deculturalization, mass removal from lands, and violent displacement cannot be ignored. Thus the deep emotional stress and historical group trauma cannot be overlooked.

Again, this book and its authors sought to be intentional in looking at student groups that deserve humanizing schools that affirm them and inspire them, schools that create learning spaces that do not require alienating their ways of speaking, thinking, communicating, being, and learning. Fighters for educational justice must also remember that there will always be resistance to efforts for educational transformation. In many of our school communities across the country, there remains an enduring belief that schools are working just fine and that those on the margins have no one but themselves to blame. Arguments that various populations lack the grit, the mental aptitude, the caregivers, or the basic desire and motivation to learn are entrenched in the minds of many educators. Thus this work is not for the meek, the weak of heart, or the thin skinned. Raising issues around equity, racism, xenophobia, and exclusion can trigger emotions, challenge certain types of privilege, evoke intense resistance, and cause harsh tensions among coworkers. Because of this, forming strategic alliances with like-minded allies is vital to this transformation. The work is heavy, stressful, tiring, and alienating at times, but it is the right thing to do.

To restate the obvious, the work of helping all students thrive will not be easy. It will not happen overnight, and it is not predicated on simplistic "to do" lists. This work requires serious learning, reading, reflecting about, and experiencing the history, community, and schooling of marginalized people—namely, people of color, women and girls, economically disadvantaged families and individuals, Muslims, members of the LGBTQ community, individuals with disabilities, gender-nonconforming people, and undocumented children and youth. Education scholar Bettina Love eloquently states the challenge before us: "When you understand how hard it is to fight for educational justice, you know that there are no shortcuts and no gimmicks; you know this to be true deep in your soul, which brings both frustration and determination. Educational justice is going to take people power."[2]

Ensuring that all children thrive requires us as members of the educational community to be introspective about how the privileged aspects of our identities must be understood so that we do better, and are better. It requires all educators to be reflective, and dedicated to improving leadership, practice, policy, and research that are concerned with all students, but in particular those often overlooked and underserved. This work requires all stakeholders to cease the blame game that has plagued education for too long. Each party must be honest, accountable, insightful, and careful about how we can all be better, do better, and educate better in a manner that speaks to our democratic ideals of opportunity, fairness, righteousness, equality, and justice. Not only should we believe that all students are deserving of a meaningful and affirming education, but we should keep fighting, struggling, protesting, praying, reflecting, voting, and working until a humanizing education is the norm for all students. Our students are worth the fight and the sacrifice.

Notes

Chapter 1

1. Banks, J. A. (2019). *An introduction to multicultural education* (6th ed.). New York, NY: Pearson.
2. US Department of Education, National Center for Education Statistics, Common Core of Data. (2016). State nonfiscal survey of public elementary and secondary education, 2003–04 and 2013–14, https://nces.ed.gov/ccd/stnfis.asp; National elementary and secondary enrollment projection model, 1972 through 2025; see also *Digest of education statistics 2015*, table 203.50, https://nces.ed.gov/programs/raceindicators/indicator_rbb.asp
3. Reardon, S. F., & Hinze-Pifer, R. (2017). *Test score growth among Chicago public school students, 2009–2014.* Palo Alto, CA: Stanford Center for Policy Analysis.
4. Milner, H. R., IV. (2015). *Rac(e)ing to class: Confronting poverty and race in schools and classrooms.* Cambridge, MA: Harvard Education Press.
5. Banks, *Introduction to multicultural education.*
6. McFarland, J., Hussar, B., de Brey, C., & Snyder, T. (2017). *The conditions of education 2017.* Washington, DC: National Center for Education Statistics. Retrieved from https://nces.ed.gov/pubs2017/2017144.pdf
7. Howard, T. C. (2010). *Why race and culture matter in schools: Closing the achievement gap in America's classrooms.* New York, NY: Teachers College Press.
8. Ladson-Billings, G. (2006). From the achievement gap to the education debt: Understanding achievement in U.S. schools. *Educational Researcher, 35,* 3–12.
9. Milner, *Rac(e)ing to class.*
10. Eddo-Lodge, R. (2017). *Why I'm no longer talking to white people about race* (p. 85). London: Bloomsbury Circus.
11. Gershenson, S., Hart, C.M.D., Lindsay, C. A., & Papageorge, N.W. (2017). *The long-run impacts of same-race teachers* (p. 35). Bonn, Germany: IZA–Institute of Labor Economics.
12. Gay, G. (2000). *Culturally responsive teaching* (p. 205). New York, NY: Teachers College Press.

13. Howard, J. R., McCall, T., and Howard, T. C. (2019). *No academics without relationships.* Portsmouth, NH: Heinemann.

14. Ladson-Billings, G. (2009). *The dreamkeepers: Successful teachers of African American children* (2nd ed.). San Francisco, CA: Jossey-Bass; Milner, H. R. (2010). *Start where you are but don't stay there: Understanding diversity, opportunity gaps, and teaching in today's classrooms.* Cambridge, MA: Harvard Education Press.

15. Ullucci, K., & Beatty, D. (2011). Exposing color blindness/grounding color consciousness: Challenges for teacher education, *Urban Education 46,* 1195–1225.

16. Ibid., p. 1196.

17. Howard, T. C., & Milner, H. R. (2014). Teacher preparation for urban schools. In H. R. Milner & K. Lomotey (Eds.), *Handbook of urban education* (pp. 199–216). New York, NY: Routledge.

18. Howard, *Why race and culture matter.*

19. Yosso, T. J. (2005). Whose culture has capital? A critical race theory discussion of community cultural wealth. *Race, Ethnicity and Education, 8,* 69–91.

20. Banks, *Introduction to multicultural education,* p. 91.

21. Erickson, F. (2012). Culture and education. In J. Banks (Ed.), *Encyclopedia of diversity in education* (pp. 560–569). Thousand Oaks, CA: Sage Publications.

22. Gay, *Culturally responsive teaching,* p. 105.

23. Gay, G., & Howard, T. (2001). Multicultural teacher education for the 21st century. *Teacher Educator, 36*(1), 1–16.

24. Milner, *Start where you are.*

Chapter 2

1. Child Welfare Information Gateway. (2014). Parenting a child who has experienced trauma. Washington, DC: US Department of Health and Human Services, Children's Bureau. Retrieved from https://www.childwelfare.gov/pubPDFs/child-trauma.pdf

2. What is trauma? (n.d.). *Early Childhood Mental Health.* Retrieved from https://dmh.mo.gov/healthykids/providers/trauma.html

3. Ibid.

4. Trauma types. (n.d.). National Child Traumatic Stress Network. Retrieved from www.nctsn.org/what-is-child-trauma/trauma-types

5. Heart, M. Y. (2003). The historical trauma response among natives and its relationship with substance abuse: A Lakota illustration. *Journal of Psychoactive Drugs, 35*(1), 7–13.

6. Bombay, A., Matheson, K., & Anisman, H. (2009). Intergenerational trauma: Convergence of multiple processes among First Nations peoples in Canada. *Journal of Aboriginal Health, 5*(3), 6–47.

7. Pickens, I. B., Siegfried, C. B., Surko, M., & Dierkhising, C. B. (2016). *Victimization and juvenile offending*. Los Angeles, CA: National Child Traumatic Stress Network.

8. Egger, H. L., & Angold, A. (2006). Common emotional and behavioral disorders in preschool children: Presentation, nosology, and epidemiology. *Journal of Child Psychology and Psychiatry, 47,* 313–337.

9. National Child Traumatic Stress Network Schools Committee. (2008). *Child trauma toolkit for educators*. Los Angeles, CA: Author.

10. Childhelp. (2013). Child abuse statistics & facts. Retrieved from https://www.childhelp.org/child-abuse-statistics/

11. Hepworth, D. H., Rooney, R. H., Rooney, G. D., & Strom-Gottfried, K. (2017). *Direct social work practice: Theory and skills* (10th ed., p. 233). Boston, MA: Cengage Learning.

12. Finkelhor, D., Turner, H., Ormrod, R. K., & Hamby, S. (2011). *Poly-victimization: Children's exposure to multiple types of violence, crime, and abuse.* Washington, DC: Office of Juvenile Justice and Delinquency Prevention.

13. Early care and education can help young children overcome trauma. (2017). Retrieved from https://www.childtrends.org/early-care-education-can-help-young-children-overcome-trauma

14. Felitti, V. J., Anda, R. F., Nordenberg, D., Williamson, D. F., Spitz, A. M., Edwards, V., & Marks, J. S. (1998). Relationship of childhood abuse and household dysfunction to many of the leading causes of death in adults. *American Journal of Preventive Medicine, 14,* 245–258.

15. Harris, N. B. (2018). *The deepest well: Healing the long-term effects of childhood adversity.* New York, NY: Houghton Mifflin Harcourt.

16. National Center for Education Statistics. (2019, February). Indicator 6: Elementary and secondary enrollment. Retrieved from https://nces.ed.gov/programs/raceindicators/indicator_rbb.asp

17. Findings from the Philadelphia Urban ACE Survey. (2013, September 18). Robert Woods Johnson Foundation. Retrieved from https://www.rwjf.org/en/library/research/2013/09/findings-from-the-philadelphia-urban-ace-survey.html

18. Souers, K., & Hall, P. (2016). *Fostering resilient learners: Strategies for creating a trauma-sensitive classroom.* Alexandria, VA: ASCD.

19. Felitti et al., Relationship of childhood abuse and household dysfunction.

20. Harris, *Deepest well.*

21. National Child Traumatic Stress Network. (n.d.). Think trauma: A training for staff in juvenile justice residential settings. Retrieved from https://learn.nctsn.org/pluginfile.php/180995/mod_resource/content/1/Think-Trauma_Module3_FacilitatorGuide.pdf

22. Pritzker, K. (Producer), & Redford, J. (Director). (2015). *Paper tigers* [Motion picture]. United States: KPJR. Retrieved from www.papertigersmovie.com

23. Blodgett, C. (2012, July 30). *How adverse childhood experiences and trauma impact school engagement.* Presentation delivered at Becca Conference, Spokane, Washington.
24. Harris, *Deepest well.*
25. Craig, S. E. (2016). *Trauma-sensitive schools: Learning communities transforming children's lives, K–5.* New York, NY: Teachers College Press.
26. LACOE/ETN [Screen name]. (2018, September 27). *Creating trauma- and resiliency-informed schools: Dr. Audra Langley* [Video file]. Retrieved from https://www.youtube.com/watch?v=sJQxoVOapsM
27. Michelon, P. (2008, February 26). Brain plasticity: How learning changes your brain. [Blog post]. Retrieved from https://sharpbrains.com/blog/2008/02/26/brain-plasticity-how-learning-changes-your-brain/
28. Souers & Hall, *Fostering resilient learners.*
29. Boyle, G. (2014). *Tattoos on the heart: The power of boundless compassion.* Winnipeg: Manitoba Education and Advanced Learning, Alternate Formats Library.
30. Cassetta, G., & Sawyer, B. (2013). *No more taking away recess and other problematic discipline procedures.* Portsmouth, NH: Heinemann.
31. Bailey, B. (2018). Understanding trauma: Reaching and teaching children with trauma [Video webinar]. Available at http://consciousdiscipline.com
32. Ibid.
33. California State University. (n.d.). Assisting students in distress. Los Angeles: Author. Retrieved from calstate.edu/red-folder
34. Ibid.
35. Smith, D., Fisher, D., & Frey, N. (2015). *Better than carrots or sticks: Restorative practices for positive classroom management.* Alexandria, VA: ASCD.
36. Shalaby, C. (2017). *Troublemakers: Lessons in freedom from young children at school.* New York, NY: New Press.

Chapter 3

1. Watson, K. T., & Pérez Huber, L. (2016). *Micro in name only: Looking back to move forward in microaggressions research* (Research Briefs, No. 3). Center for Critical Race Studies at UCLA.
2. Rudd, T. (2014). *Racial disproportionality in school discipline: Implicit bias is heavily implicated* (Kirwan Institute Issue Brief), 1–8. Retrieved from http://kirwaninstitute.osu.edu/wp-content/uploads/2014/02/racial-disproportionality-schools-02.pdf
3. Kahn, J. (2017). *Race on the brain: What implicit bias gets wrong about the struggle for racial justice.* New York, NY: Columbia University Press.
4. Banaji, M. R., & Greenwald, A. G. (2013). *Blindspot: Hidden biases of good people.* New York, NY: Random House.
5. Ibid.

6. Rudd, *Racial disproportionality.*
7. Rudd, T. (2012, Aug. 11). *Implicit racial bias: Implications for education and other critical opportunity domains.* Presentation to the National Association for the Education of African American Children with Learning Disabilities.
8. Wilson, J. P., Hugenberg, K., & Rule, N. O. (2017). Racial bias in judgments of physical size and formidability: From size to threat. *Journal of Personality and Social Psychology, 113*(1), 59–80.
9. Holbrook, C., Fessler, D. M., & Navarrete, C. D. (2016). Looming large in others' eyes: Racial stereotypes illuminate dual adaptations for representing threat versus prestige as physical size. *Journal of Evolution and Human Behavior, 37*(1), 67–78.
10. Goff, P. A., Jackson, M. C., Allison, B., Di Leone, L., Culotta, M., & DiTomasso, N. A. (2014). The essence of innocence: Consequences of dehumanizing black children. *Journal of Personality and Social Psychology, 106,* 526–545.
11. Hoffman, K. M., Trawalter, S., Axt, J. R., & Oliver, M. N. (2016). Racial bias in pain assessment and treatment recommendations, and false beliefs about biological differences between blacks and whites. *Proceedings of the National Academy of Sciences, 113,* 4296–4301.
12. Pérez Huber, L., & Solórzano, D. G. (2015). *Microaggressions: What they are, what they are not, and why they matter* (Latino Policy & Issues Brief, No. 30). UCLA Chicano Studies Research Center.
13. Pierce, C. M. (1969). Is bigotry the basis of the medical problems of the ghetto? In J. C. Norman (Ed.), *Medicine in the ghetto* (pp. 301–312). New York, NY: Meredith.
14. Solórzano, D. G., Ceja, M., & Yosso, T. (2000) Critical race theory, racial microaggressions and campus racial climate: The experiences of African-American college students. *Journal of Negro Education, 69*(1/2), 60–73.
15. Berry, C. D., & Duke, B. (Producers & Directors). (2011). *Dark girls* [Motion picture]. United States: Urban Winter Entertainment. http://officialdarkgirlsmovie.com/about/
16. Banaji & Greenwald, *Blindspot.*
17. Pérez Huber & Solórzano, *Microaggressions.*
18. Smith, E. J., & Harper, S. R. (2015). *Disproportionate impact of K-12 school suspension and expulsion on Black students in southern states.* Philadelphia, PA: University of Pennsylvania, Center for the Study of Race and Equity in Education. Retrieved from www.gse.upenn.edu/equity/sites/gse.upenn.edu.equity/files/publications/Smith_ Harper_Report.pdf
19. Epstein, R., Blake, J., & González, T. (2017). *Girlhood interrupted: The erasure of black girls' childhood.* Center on Poverty and Inequality. Retrieved from http://www.law.georgetown.edu/academics/centers-institutes/povertyinequality/upload/girlhood-interrupted.pdf

20. Heitzeg, N. A. (2009). Education or incarceration: Zero tolerance policies and the school to prison pipeline. *Forum on Public Policy Online, 2009*(2). (ERIC Document Reproduction Service No. EJ870 076).

21. Kohli, R., & Solórzano, D. G. (2012). Teachers, please learn our names! Racial microaggressions and the K–12 classroom. *Race, Ethnicity and Education, 15,* 441–462. doi:10.1080/13613324.2012.674026

22. Bishop, J. M. (2017). Mapping violence, naming life: A history of anti-black oppression in the higher education system. *International Journal of Qualitative Studies in Education, 30,* 711–727. doi:10.1080/09518398 .2017.1350299

23. Kohli & Solórzano. Teachers, please learn our names!

24. Heitzeg, Education or incarceration.

25. Adam, E. K., Heissel, J. A., Zeiders, K. H., Richeson, J. A., Ross, E. C., Ehrlich, K. B., . . . Peck, S. C. (2015). Developmental histories of perceived racial discrimination and diurnal cortisol profiles in adulthood: A 20-year prospective study. *Journal of Psychoneuroendocrinology, 62,* 279–291.

26. Watson, K. T. (2018). *Revealing cuts beneath skin: Black men and the bio-psychosocial impact of racial microaggressions.* Manuscript in preparation.

27. Bell, D. (1992). *The space traders: Faces at the bottom of the well.* New York, NY: Basic Books.

28. Bell, D. (2004). *Silent covenants:* Brown v. Board of Education *and the unfulfilled hopes for racial reform.* New York, NY: Oxford University Press.

29. Maxwell, L. (2014, August 19). U.S. school enrollment hits majority-minority milestone. *Education Week.* Retrieved from http://www .edweek.org/ew/articles/2014/08/20/01demographics.h34.html

30. Tatum, B. D. (1997). *Why are all the black kids sitting together in the cafeteria? And other conversations about race.* New York, NY: Basic Books.

31. Pierce, C. (1970). Offensive mechanisms. In F. B. Barbour (Ed.), *The black seventies* (pp. 265–282). Boston, MA: Porter Sargent.

32. Solórzano, D. G., Pérez Huber, L., & Huber-Verjan, L. (in press). Theorizing racial microaffirmations across three generations of critical race scholars. *University of Miami Social Justice Law Review.*

33. Pérez Huber, L. (2018, June). Racial microaffirmations as a response to microaggressions (Research Brief No. 15). Center for Critical Race Studies at UCLA.

Chapter 4

1. Paris, D., & Alim, H. S. (2014). What are we seeking to sustain through culturally sustaining pedagogy? A loving critique forward. *Harvard Educational Review, 84*(1), 85–100; Gay, G. (2000). *Culturally responsive teaching: Theory, research, and practice.* New York, NY: Teachers College Press.

2. Banks, J. (2006). *Race, culture, and education: The selected works of James A. Banks.* London and New York: Routledge; Howard, T. C. (2010). *Why race and culture matter in schools: Closing the achievement gap in America's classrooms.* New York, NY: Teachers College Press.

3. Gordon, N. (2017, September 20). *Race, poverty, and interpreting overrepresentation in special education.* Retrieved from https://www.brookings.edu/research/race-poverty-and-interpreting-overrepresentation-in-special-education/; Cardichon, J. (2014, August 5). *How to address the over-representation of students of color in special education.* Alliance for Excellent Education. Retrieved from https://all4ed.org/how-to-address-the-over-representation-of-students-of-color-in-special-education/; and Blanchett, W. (2006). Disproportionate representation of African American students in special education: Acknowledging the role of white privilege and racism. *Educational Researcher, 35*(6), 24–28.

4. Delgato-Gaitan, C., & Trueba, H. (1991). *Crossing cultural borders: Education for immigrant families in America.* New York, NY: Falmer; Gay, *Culturally responsive teaching.*

5. Ladson-Billings, G. (1994). *The dreamkeepers: Successful teachers of African American children.* San Francisco, CA: Jossey-Bass.

6. Gay, G. (2002) Preparing for culturally responsive teaching. *Journal of Teacher Education, 53*(2), 107, 106–116.

7. Hammond, Z. (2015). *Culturally responsive teaching and the brain.* Thousand Oaks, CA: Corwin Press.

8. Gay, G. (2018). *Culturally responsive teaching: Theory, research, and practice* (3rd ed.). New York, NY: Teachers College Press.

9. Ibid., p. 58.

10. Bryk, A., & Schneider, B. (2003). Trust in schools: A core resource for school reform. *Educational Leadership, 60*(6), 40–45.

11. Gutierrez, R. (2009). Embracing the inherent tensions in teaching mathematics from an equity stance. *Democracy & Education, 18*(3), 9–16.

12. Hammond, *Culturally responsive teaching and the brain*; Hollie, S. (2011). *Culturally and linguistically responsive teaching and learning.* Huntington Beach, CA: Shell Education.

Chapter 5

1. Shonkoff, J., & Phillips, D. (2000). *From neurons to neighborhoods: The science of early childhood development.* Washington, DC: National Academies Press.

2. Katz, P. A., & Kofkin, J. A. (1997). Race, gender, and young children. In S. S. Luthar, J. A. Burack, D. Cicchetti, & J. R. Weisz (Eds.), *Developmental psychopathology: Perspectives on adjustment, risk, and disorder* (pp. 51–74). New York, NY: Cambridge University Press; Van Ausdale, D., &

Feagin, J. R. (2001). *The first R: How children learn race and racism.* Lanham, MD: Rowman & Littlefield.

3. Colby, S. L., & Ortman, J. M. (2015). *Projections of the size and composition of the U.S. population: 2014–2060.* Washington, DC: US Census Bureau.

4. Hollins, E. R., & Guzman, M. T. (2005). Research on preparing teachers for diverse populations. In M. Cochran-Smith & K. M. Zeichner (Eds.), *Studying teacher education: The report of the AERA Panel on Research and Teacher Education* (pp. 477–548). Mahwah, NJ: Erlbaum.

5. Howard, T. C., & Milner H. R., IV. (2014). Teacher preparation for urban schools. In H. R. Milner IV & K. Lomotey (Eds.), *Handbook of urban education* (pp. 199–216). New York, NY: Routledge.

6. Katz & Kofkin, Race, gender, and young children.

7. Ibid.

8. Pahlke, E., Bigler, R. S., & Suizzo, M. A. (2012). Relations between colorblind socialization and children's racial bias: Evidence from European American mothers and their preschool children. *Child Development, 83,* 1164–1179.

9. Boykin, A. W., & Ellison, C. M. (1995). The multiple ecologies of black youth socialization: An Afrocentric analysis. In R. L. Taylor (Ed.), *African-American youth: Their social and economic status in the United States* (pp. 93–128). Westport, CT: Praeger.

10. Peters, M. F., & Massey, G. (1983). Mundane extreme environmental stress in family stress theories: The case of black families in white America. *Marriage & Family Review, 6,* 193–218.

11. Hughes, D., & Johnson, D. (2001). Correlates in children's experiences of parents' racial socialization behaviors. *Journal of Marriage and Family, 63,* 981–995.

12. Pahlke et al., Relations between colorblind socialization and children's racial bias.

13. Ibid.

14. Ibid.

15. Hughes, J. M., Bigler, R. S., & Levy, S. R. (2007). Consequences of learning about historical racism among European American and African American children. *Child Development, 78,* 1685–1705.

16. Vittrup, B., & Holden, G. W. (2011). Exploring the impact of educational television and parent–child discussions on children's racial attitudes. *Analyses of Social Issues and Public Policy, 11*(1), 82–104.

17. Gay, G., & Howard, T. C. (2000). Multicultural teacher education for the 21st century. *Teacher Educator, 36*(1), 1–16.

18. Tenore, F. B., Dunn, A. C., Laughter, J. C., & Milner, H. R. (2010). Teacher candidate selection, recruitment, and induction. In V. Hill-Jackson & C. W. Lewis (Eds.), *Transforming teacher education: What went wrong with teacher training and how we can fix it* (pp. 93–118). Sterling, VA: Stylus;

Zumwalt, K., & Craig, E. (2005). Teachers' characteristics: Research on the demographic profile. In M. Cochran-Smith & K. M. Zeichner (Eds.), *Studying teacher education: The report of the AERA Panel on Research and Teacher Education* (pp. 111–156). Mahwah, NJ: Erlbaum.

19. Tenore et al., Teacher candidate selection, recruitment, and induction.
20. Causey, V. E., Thomas, C. D., & Armento, B. J. (2000). Cultural diversity is basically a foreign term to me: The challenges of diversity for preservice teacher education. *Teaching and Teacher Education, 16,* 33–45.
21. Harro, B. (2000). The cycle of socialization. In M. Adams, W. J. Blumenfeld, R. Castaneda, H. W. Hackman, M. L. Peters, & X. Zúñiga (Eds.), *Readings for diversity and social justice* (pp. 15–21). New York, NY: Routledge.
22. US Department of Education, Office of Civil Rights. (2016). *2013–2014 civil rights data collection: Key data highlights on equity and opportunity gaps in our nation's public schools.* Retrieved from http://www2.ed.gov/about/offices/list/ocr/docs/crdc-2013-14.html
23. Gilliam, W. S., Maupin, A. N., Reyes, C. R., Accavitti, M., & Shic, F. (2016, September). Do early educators' implicit biases regarding sex and race relate to behavior expectations and recommendations of preschool expulsions and suspensions? (Research Study Brief). New Haven, CT: Yale Child Study Center, Yale University.
24. Cherng, H. Y. (2016). Is all classroom conduct equal? Teacher contact with parents of racial/ethnic minority and immigrant adolescents. *Teachers College Record, 118*(11), 1–32.
25. Derman-Sparks, L., & Ramsey, P. G. (2011). *What if all the kids are white? Anti-bias multicultural education with young children and families.* New York, NY: Teachers College Press, p. 7.
26. Aboud, F. E., & Doyle, A. B. (1996). Parental and peer influences on children's racial attitudes. *International Journal of Intercultural Relations, 20,* 371–383; Castelli, L., Zogmaister, C., & Tomelleri, S. (2009). The transmission of racial attitudes within the family. *Developmental Psychology, 45,* 586–591.
27. Vezzali, L., Giovannini, D., & Capozza, D. (2012). Social antecedents of children's implicit prejudice: Direct contact, extended contact, explicit and implicit teachers' prejudice. *European Journal of Developmental Psychology, 9,* 569–581.
28. Carter, R. T., & Goodwin, A. L. (1994). Racial identity and education. *Review of Research in Education, 20,* 291–336.
29. Sanders, K., & Downer, J. (2012). Predicting acceptance of diversity in pre-kindergarten classrooms. *Early Childhood Research Quarterly, 27,* 503–511.
30. Ibid.
31. Han, H. S., West-Olatunji, C., & Thomas, M. S. (2010). Use of racial development identity theory to explore cultural competence among early

childhood educators. *Journal of Southeastern Regional Association for Teacher Educators, 20*(1), 1–11.

32. Staats, C. (2016). Understanding implicit bias: What educators should know. *American Educator, 39*(4), 29–43.

33. Pascalis, O., & Slater, A. (2003). *The development of face processing in infancy and early childhood: Current perspectives.* Hauppauge, NY: Nova Science.

34. Baron, A. S. (2015). Constraints on the development of implicit intergroup attitudes. *Child Development Perspectives, 9*(1), 50–54.

35. Baron, A. S., & Banaji, M. R. (2006). The development of implicit attitudes: Evidence of race evaluations from ages 6 and 10 and adulthood. *Psychological Science, 17*(1), 53–58.

36. Lai, C. K., Marini, M., Lehr, S. A., Cerruti, C., Shin, J.E.L., Joy-Gaba, J. A., . . . Frazier, R. S. (2014). Reducing implicit racial preferences: I. A comparative investigation of 17 interventions. *Journal of Experimental Psychology: General, 143,* 1765–1785.

37. Gregg, A. P., Seibt, B., & Banaji, M. R. (2006). Easier done than undone: Asymmetry in the malleability of implicit preferences. *Journal of Personality and Social Psychology, 90*(1), 1–20.

38. Sleeter, C. E., & Owuor, J. (2011). Research on the impact of teacher preparation to teach diverse students: The research we have and the research we need. *Action in Teacher Education, 33,* 524–537; Howard, T. C. (2003). Culturally relevant pedagogy: Ingredients for critical teacher reflection. *Theory into Practice, 42,* 195–202; and Gay & Howard, Multicultural teacher education for the 21st century.

39. Darling-Hammond, L. (2000). How teacher education matters. *Journal of Teacher Education, 51,* 166–173; Howard, Culturally relevant pedagogy; and Lynn, M., & Smith-Maddox, R. (2007). Preservice teacher inquiry: Creating a space to dialogue about becoming a social justice educator. *Teaching and Teacher Education, 23*(1), 94–105.

40. Derman-Sparks & Ramsey, *What if all the kids are white?*

41. Devine, P. G., Forscher, P. S., Austin, A. J., & Cox, W. T. (2012). Long-term reduction in implicit race bias: A prejudice habit-breaking intervention. *Journal of Experimental Social Psychology, 48,* 1267–1278.

42. Moll, L. C., Amanti, C., Neff, D., & Gonzalez, N. (1992). Funds of knowledge for teaching: Using a qualitative approach to connect homes and classrooms. *Theory into Practice, 31,* 132–141.

43. Galinsky, A. D., & Moskowitz, G. B. (2000). Perspective-taking: Decreasing stereotype expression, stereotype accessibility, and in-group favoritism. *Journal of Personality and Social Psychology, 78,* 708–724.

44. Fort, D. C., & Varney, H. L. (1989). How students see scientists: Mostly male, mostly white, and mostly benevolent. *Science and Children, 26*(8), 8–13.

45. Banaji, M. R., & Greenwald, A. G. (2016). *Blindspot: Hidden biases of good people*. New York, NY: Bantam.
46. Ibid.
47. Dasgupta, N., & Asgari, S. (2004). Seeing is believing: Exposure to counterstereotypic women leaders and its effect on the malleability of automatic gender stereotyping. *Journal of Experimental Social Psychology, 40*, 642–658.
48. Derman-Sparks, L., & Edwards, J. O. (2010). *Anti-bias education for young children and ourselves*. Washington, DC: National Association for the Education of Young Children, p. 43.
49. Derman-Sparks and Edwards, *Anti-bias education*.
50. Devine et al., Long-term reduction in implicit race bias.
51. Hammond, Z. (2015). *Culturally responsive teaching and the brain: Promoting authentic engagement and rigor among culturally and linguistically diverse students*. Thousand Oaks, CA: Corwin Press.
52. Banaji & Greenwald, *Blindspot*.
53. Finnerty, D. (2018). Understanding unconscious bias as one more tool in the committed white teacher's equity toolkit. In E. Moore Jr., A. Michal, & M. W. Penick-Parks (Eds.), *The guide for white women who teach black boys* (pp. 55–60). Thousand Oaks, CA: Corwin Press.
54. Winkler, E. N. (2009). Children are not colorblind: How young children learn race. *PACE: Practical Approaches for Continuing Education, 3*(3), 1–8.
55. Pine, G. J., & Hilliard, A. G. (1990). Rx for racism: Imperatives for America's schools. *Phi Delta Kappan, 71*, 593–600.
56. Tatum, B. D. (2017). *Why are all the black kids sitting together in the cafeteria? And other conversations about race*. New York, NY: Basic Books, p. 86.
57. Gonzalez-Sobrino, B., & Goss, D. R. (2019). Exploring the mechanisms of racialization beyond the black–white binary. *Ethnic and Racial Studies, 42*, 505–510.

Chapter 6

1. National Center for Education Statistics. (n.d.). Retrieved from https://nces.ed.gov/pubs2019/2019144.pdf; McFarland, J., Hussar, B., Zhang, J., Wang, X., Wang, K., Hein, S., Diliberti, M., Forrest Cataldi, E., Bullock Mann, F., & Barmer, A. (2019). *The condition of education 2019* (NCES 2019-144; p. 150). US Department of Education. Washington, DC: National Center for Education Statistics. Retrieved from https://nces.ed.gov/pubsearch/pubsinfo.asp?pubid=2019144
2. Ascher, C., & Maguire, C. (2007). *Beating the odds: How thirteen NYC schools bring low-performing ninth-graders to timely graduation and college enrollment*. Providence, RI: Annenberg Institute for School Reform.

3. Adelman, C. 2006. *The toolbox revisited: Paths to degree completion from high school through college.* Washington, DC: US Department of Education.
4. Conley, D. T. (2008). *College knowledge: What it really takes for students to succeed and what we can do to get them ready.* Hoboken, NJ: Wiley.
5. Ladson-Billings, G. (1995). But that's just good teaching! The case for culturally relevant pedagogy. *Theory into Practice, 34,* 159–165.
6. Ladson-Billings, G. (2009). *The dreamkeepers: Successful teachers of African American children* (2nd ed.). San Francisco, CA: Jossey-Bass.
7. Haberman, M. (1991). Pedagogy of poverty versus good teaching. *Phi Delta Kappan, 73,* 290–294; Hodges, H. (2001). Overcoming a pedagogy of power. In R. W. Cole (Ed.), *More strategies for educating everybody's children* (pp. 1–9). Alexandria, VA: ASCD.
8. Werner, E. E., & Smith, R. S. (1989). *Vulnerable but invincible: A longitudinal study of resilient children and youth.* New York, NY: Adams Bannister Cox; Werner, E. E., & Smith, R. S. (1992). Overcoming the odds: High-risk children from birth to adulthood. Ithaca, NY: Cornell University Press; and Benard, B. (1995). *Fostering resilience in children.* (ERIC Document Reproduction Service No. ED386 327).
9. Noddings, N. (1998). Caring and competence. *Yearbook of the National Society for the Study of Education, 1,* 205–220; Benard, *Fostering resilience in children.*
10. Benard, B. (1992). *Mentoring programs for urban youth: Handle with care.* (ERIC Document Reproduction Service No. ED349 368); Patterson, J. K. (2012). *The road to the top: How educationally resilient black students defied the odds and earned admission to a selective university* (Unpublished doctoral dissertation). University of California, Los Angeles.

Chapter 7

1. Solórzano, D. G., & Yosso, T. (2004). From racial stereotyping and deficit discourse toward a critical race theory of teacher education. In W. De la Torre, L. Rubalcalva, & B. Cabello (Eds.), *Urban education in America: A critical perspective* (pp. 67–81). Dubuque, IA: Kendall/Hunt.
2. Zins, J. E., & Elias, M. J. (2007). Social and emotional learning: Promoting the development of all students. *Journal of Educational and Psychological Consultation, 17,* 233.
3. Elias, M. J. (2006). The connection between academic and social-emotional learning. In M. J. Elias & H. A. Arnold (Eds.), *The educator's guide to emotional intelligence and academic achievement: Social-emotional learning in the classroom* (pp. 4–14). Thousand Oaks, CA: Corwin Press.

4. Farmer, P. E., Nizeye, B., Stulac, S., & Keshavjee, S. (2006). Structural violence and clinical medicine. *PLoS Medicine, 3,* e449.

5. Ginwright, S. (2015). *Hope and healing in urban education.* New York, NY: Routledge.

6. Duncan-Andrade, J.M.R. (2009). Note to educators: Hope required when growing roses in concrete. *Harvard Educational Review, 79,* 181–194.

7. Valdez, C. (2018, July). Flippin' the scripted curriculum: Ethnic studies inquiry in elementary education. *Race Ethnicity and Education,* p. 4. doi: 10.1080/13613324.2018.1497959

8. Freire, P. (2002). *Pedagogy of the oppressed* (p. 88). New York, NY: Continuum. (Original work published 1970)

9. Duncan-Andrade, Note to educators, p. 187.

10. Fanon, F. (2001). *The wretched of the earth* (C. Farrington, Trans.). New York, NY: Grove. (Original work published 1963)

11. X, M. (1963). *Message to the grassroots.* Retrieved from http://teachingamerican history.org/library/index.asp?document=1145

12. Martinez, A. N., Valdez, C., & Cariaga, S. (2016). Solidarity with the people: Organizing to disrupt teacher alienation. *Equity & Excellence in Education, 49,* 300–313.

13. Bartolome, L. (1994). Beyond the methods fetish: Toward a humanizing pedagogy. *Harvard Educational Review, 64,*173–194.

14. Freire, *Pedagogy of the oppressed.*

15. Solórzano & Yosso, From racial stereotyping and deficit discourse.

16. Freire, *Pedagogy of the oppressed,* p. 48.

17. This case study draws heavily from Camangian, P. R. (2015). Teaching like lives depend on it: Agitate, arouse, inspire. *Urban Education, 50*(4), 424–453.

18. Zins & Elias, Social and emotional learning.

19. Akom, A. (2003). Reexamining resistance as oppositional behavior: The Nation of Islam and the creation of a black achievement ideology. *Sociology of Education, 76,* 305–325.

20. Duncan-Andrade, Note to educators; Leonardo, Z., & Porter, R. K. (2010). Pedagogy of fear: Toward a Fanonian theory of "safety" in race dialogue. *Race Ethnicity and Education, 13,* 139–157.

21. Parmer, T., Arnold, M., Natt, T., Janson, C. (2004). Physical attractiveness as a process of internalized oppression and multigenerational transmission in African American families. *Family Journal, 12,* 230–242.

Chapter 8

1. NYS-TEACHS. (2018). *Data on student homelessness in NYS.* New York, NY: Advocates for Children of New York.

2. National Center for Education Statistics. (2017). *Student homelessness in urban, suburban, town, and rural districts.* Retrieved from https://nces .ed.gov/blogs/nces/post/student-homelessness-in-urban-suburban-town-and-rural-districts

3. Miller, P. M. (2011). A critical analysis of the research on student homelessness. *Review of Educational Research, 81,* 308–337. doi:10.3102/0034654311415120

4. National Center for Homeless Education. (2019). *Federal data summary school years 2015–16 to 2016–17.* Greensboro: University of North Carolina. Retrieved from https://nche.ed.gov/wp-content/uploads/2019/02/Federal-Data-Summary-SY-14.15-to-16.17-Final-Published-2.12.19.pdf

5. Hallett, R. E., & Skrla, L. (2016). *Serving students who are homeless: A resource guide for schools, districts, and educational leaders.* New York, NY: Teachers College Press.

6. Aviles de Bradley, A. (2015). *From charity to equity—Race, homelessness, and urban schools.* New York, NY: Teachers College Press.

7. Ingram, E. S., Bridgeland, J. M., Reed, B., & Atwell, M. (2017). *Hidden in plain sight: Homeless students in America's public schools.* Civic Enterprises. Retrieved from www.americaspromise.org/sites/default/files/d8/2016-12/HiddeninPlainSightFullReportFINAL_0.pdf

8. Hallett, R. E. (2012). Living doubled-up: Influence of residential environment on educational participation. *Education and Urban Society, 44,* 371–391.

9. Tyler, K. A., & Schmitz, R. M. (2018). Childhood disadvantage, social and psychological stress, and substance use among homeless youth: A life stress framework. *Youth & Society.* doi.org/10.1177/0044118X18767032

10. Mayberry, L. S., Shinn, M., Benton, J. G., & Wise, J. (2014). Families experiencing housing instability: The effects of housing programs on family routines and rituals. *American Journal of Orthopsychiatry, 84*(1), 95–109.

11. National Scientific Council on the Developing Child. (2014). *Toxic stress disrupts brain architecture.* Cambridge, MA: Harvard University. Retrieved from https://developingchild.harvard.edu/resources/wp3/

12. Kataoka, S., Langley, A., Wong, M., Baweja, S., & Stein, B. (2012). Responding to students with posttraumatic stress disorder in schools. *Child and Adolescent Psychiatric Clinics of North America, 21*(1), 119–133.

13. Ibid.

14. Miller, P. M., & Schreiber, J. (2012). Multilevel considerations of family homelessness and schooling in the recession era. *Journal of School Leadership, 22,* 147–185.

15. National Center for Homeless Education, *Federal data summary.*

16. Murphy, J. F., & Tobin, K. J. (2011). Homelessness comes to school. *Phi Delta Kappan, 93*(3), 32–37.

17. US Bureau of Labor Statistics. (2017). *Unemployment rates and earnings by educational attainment.* Retrieved from https://www.bls.gov/emp/ep_table_001.htm

18. Cowen, J. M. (2017). Who are the homeless? Student mobility and achievement in Michigan 2010–2013. *Educational Researcher, 46*(1), 33–43. doi:10.3102/0013189X17694165; Moore, J. (2005). *Collaborations of schools and social service agencies.* Greensboro, NC: National Center for Homeless Education at SERVE.

19. Smerillo, N. E., Reynolds, A. J., Temple, J. A., & Ou, S.-R. (2018). Chronic absence, eighth-grade achievement, and high school attainment in the Chicago Longitudinal Study. *Journal of School Psychology, 67,* 163–178.

20. Pappas, L. (2018). *Not reaching the door: Homeless students face many hurdles on the way to school* (p. 58). New York, NY: New York City Independent Budget Office.

21. Child Trends Databank. (2015). Homeless children and youth. Retrieved from https://www.childtrends.org/?indicators=homeless-children-and-youth

22. Edwards, E. J., & Noguera, P. A. (in press). Seeing our most vulnerable homeless students: The impact of structural racism on the education of black homeless youth in the United States. In K. Seaman & R. Rashawn (Eds.), *Structural racism and the root causes of prejudice.* Berkeley, CA: University of California Press.

23. Texas Education Agency. (2018). *Enrollment in Texas public schools, 2017–18* (Document No. GE18 601 06). Austin: Author.

24. Conroy, S. J., & Heer, D. M. (2003). Hidden Hispanic homelessness in Los Angeles: The "Latino paradox" revisited. *Hispanic Journal of Behavioral Sciences, 25,* 530–538. doi:10.1177/0739986303258126

25. Durso, L. E., & Gates, G. J. (2012). *Serving our youth: Findings from a national survey of services providers working with lesbian, gay, bisexual and transgender youth who are homeless or at risk of becoming homeless.* Los Angeles, CA: Williams Institute with True Colors Fund and Palette Fund. Retrieved from https://escholarship.org/uc/item/80x75033

26. Morton, M. H., Samuels, G., Dworsky, A., & Patel, S. (2018). *Missed opportunities: LGBTQ youth homelessness in America.* Chicago: Chaplin Hall at the University of Chicago.

27. Durso & Gates, Serving our youth.

28. Ingram et al., *Hidden in plain sight.*

29. Hornor, G. (2015). Childhood trauma exposure and toxic stress: What the PNP needs to know. *Journal of Pediatric Health Care, 29,* 191–198. doi:10.1016/j.pedhc.2014.09.006

30. Edwards, E. J., & Noguera, P. A. (in press). Seeing our most vulnerable homeless students: Analyzing the impact of structural racism on the education of black homeless youth in the United States. In R. Ray &

H. Mahmoudi (Eds.), *Structural racism and the root causes of prejudice.* Berkeley: University of California Press.

31. Ingram et al., *Hidden in plain sight.*

Conclusion

1. Maslow, A. (1943). A theory of motivation. *Psychological Review, 50,* 370–396.

2. Love, B. L. (2019). *We want to do more than survive: Abolitionist teaching and the pursuit of educational freedom.* Boston, MA: Beach Press.

Index

Pledge of Allegiance, critique of, lesson involving, 110

police brutality: critique of, lesson involving, 85, *86*; trauma from, points of view shaped by, understanding, 130

police shootings, 113

political climate, current, 9, 56

population figures, 2–3, 4, 25, 95–96

positionality: defining, 77; teachers investigating and examining own, *75*, 77, 78, 79, 90

positive role models, teachers as, 110

post-enslavement, period of, 51, 52

poverty: focus on, xxiv; importance of understanding effects of, xxi, xxiv; student population figures and, 2

power inequities, analyzing, 129

power struggles, avoiding, 41

praise, providing, 38–39

precise time, 83

"problem" children, labeled as. *See* labeling students, issue with

problem solvers versus problem posers, 70

professional development (PD) sessions, providing, to address student homelessness, 163

Promoting Racial Literacy in Schools: Differences That Make a Difference (Stevenson), 17–18

psychological indicators, 33

public praising, 38–39

public shaming, rejection of, 38

punitive discipline practices, 29, 38

Pushout: The Criminalization of Black Girls in Schools (Morris), 17

Q

questions: existential, exploring, 130; guiding, use of, in SEL practice, 134, 136; taking notice of behaviors and asking, 33, 34; in What Would You Do? scenarios, 12–13, 53, 54, 166, 167

R

race: academic disparities and, 4–5; being mindful of, 10; conversations about, need for, at an early age, 94–95; culture versus, 11–12, 71; deficit ideology of, emergence of, 69; defining, 5; discomfort in talking about, 8–9, 15, 94–95, 113; examining role of, xix; fears around, political climate intensifying, 9; focus on, xxiv; importance of understanding effects of, xxi, xxii, xxiv, 5–8, 14; invisibility of, *72*; learning more about, 15; research on, issue of Black/White binary in, 104

race relations, improving, 95

Rac(e)ing to Class (Milner), 16

racial attitudes, development of, 94–95

racial conditioning, implicit, 99

racial hierarchy, 5

racial identity development model, 98. *See also* identity

racial knowledge, as requisite, 8, 94

racial literacy: benefits of developing, 1–2, 10; culturally relevant pedagogy requiring, 112; importance of, xxii, 8; key takeaways on, 14; and questions from the field, 14–15; resources on, 15–18; scenarios to reflect on, 12–13

racial microaffirmations, 61–62, 63, 67

WITHDRAWN FROM LIBRARY

CARROLL COUNTY
NOV   2020
PUBLIC LIBRARY